Business Studies

Other titles in this series

Business Calculations
Business Communication
Business Law
The Business of Government

Business Studies

Mark Juby, BSc, PGCE, is Head of the Business Studies Department, Finham Park School, Coventry. He is currently involved with TVE Modular Business Studies courses and is also chief examiner for the Understanding Industrial Society exam for the Midlands Exam Group.

Business Studies

Mark Juby

Chambers Commerce Series

© Mark Juby 1987

Published by W & R Chambers Ltd Edinburgh, 1987

All rights reserved. No part of this publication may be reproduced or transmitted in any form or by any means, electronic or mechanical, including photocopying, recording or any information storage or retrieval system without prior permission, in writing, from the publisher.

British Library Cataloguing in Publication Data

Juby, Mark
  Business studies.—(Chambers commerce series)
  1. Business education
  I. Title
  658   HF1106

ISBN 0-550-20703-1

Typeset by Image Services Ltd, Edinburgh

Printed in Great Britain by
Richard Clay Ltd, Bungay, Suffolk

Contents

PART I   THE BUSINESS ENVIRONMENT

Chapter 1   Business Activity

1.1 Economic Activity	3
1.2 The Business Community	8
1.3 Business and its Environment	12
Test Yourself	14

Chapter 2   Business Structure and Organisation

2.1 The Sole Trader	16
2.2 Partnerships	18
2.3 Private Limited Companies (Ltd)	20
2.4 Public Limited Companies (PLC)	20
2.5 Co-operatives	21
2.6 Legal Arrangements	22
Test Yourself	24
Questions	25

Chapter 3   Internal Organisation

3.1 The Structure of a Company	26
3.2 The Production Department	27
3.3 The Finance Department	28
3.4 The Personnel Department	29
3.5 The Marketing Department	31
3.6 The Administration Department	32
3.7 Control	33
3.8 Centralisation versus Decentralisation	36
Test Yourself	38
Questions	38

PART II   BUSINESS BEHAVIOUR

Chapter 4   The Market

4.1 Finding a Market for your Product/Service	43
4.2 Selling the Product/Service	45

4.3	Consumer Protection	52
	Test Yourself	55
	Questions	56

Chapter 5 Producing the Product

5.1	Production and Specialisation	57
5.2	Production Methods	60
5.3	The Location of Industry	62
5.4	Factory Design	65
5.5	Production Control	68
5.6	Quality Control	69
5.7	Stock Control	70
	Test Yourself	76
	Questions	76

Chapter 6 Raising Capital

6.1	Start-up Capital	77
6.2	Circulating Capital	80
6.3	Fixed Capital	81
6.4	Shares	82
6.5	Issuing Shares/Going Public	84
6.6	The Big Bang	85
6.7	Other Methods of Raising Capital	86
	Test Yourself	87
	Questions	87

Chapter 7 Reporting, Planning and Control

7.1	The Balance Sheet	88
7.2	The Profit and Loss Account	93
7.3	Analysis of Accounts (Ratio Analysis)	94
7.4	Management Accounts	96
7.5	Making a Profit	99
	Test Yourself	106
	Questions	107

PART III PEOPLE AND WORK

Chapter 8 Human Needs and Work

8.1	Why People Work	111
8.2	Work and Motivation	114
8.3	Job Enrichment	117
8.4	Pay	117
8.5	Why Incomes Differ	121
8.6	Gross Pay versus Net Pay	127
	Test Yourself	130
	Questions	131

Chapter 9 Selection and Recruitment

9.1	Applying for a Job	132
9.2	Induction, Training and Staff Development	138
9.3	Promotion and Appraisal	140
9.4	Leadership	142
9.5	Communication	145
	Test Yourself	152
	Questions	152

Chapter 10 Industrial Relations

10.1	Trade Unions	153
10.2	Description of a Typical Trade Union	156
10.3	The Trades Union Congress (TUC)	157
10.4	Joint National Councils	157
10.5	Employers' Associations and the Confederation of British Industry (CBI)	158
10.6	Industrial Disputes	158
10.7	Negotiations	161
10.8	Present Issues in Industrial Relations	162
	Test Yourself	167
	Questions	168

Index 169

Preface

This book has been written as an introduction to the diversity of areas covered by the term Business Studies. The text is specifically designed to cover the GCSE National Criteria in Business Studies and the book also covers many of the key areas of the GCSE Commerce and Understanding Industrial Society Courses. The book is also suitable for a wide range of business and vocational courses that contain an element of Business Studies.

Each chapter is divided into convenient study sections. There are frequent *Tasks* suitable for both class exercises and individual study. At the end of the chapter is a *Test Yourself* exercise designed to evaluate recall of knowledge. Following this are stepped *Questions* which progress from simple recall to those involving the higher skills of comprehension, inquiry, evaluation and synthesis.

I wish to thank the Design Council and British Standards Institute for the use of their logos, Joyce Pienkowski for typing the original manuscript and Jane Freshwater for her support and encouragement in the writing of this book.

M. J.

PART I
THE BUSINESS ENVIRONMENT

Chapter 1

Business Activity

When we talk of business, different people will give the word different meanings. No two companies are the same. A business can be a newly formed one-man concern selling china mugs in a local market or a huge multi-national conglomeration employing thousands of people and manufacturing many different products.

As varied as business activity may be, we are faced with the inescapable fact that we cannot live without it. Business provides goods and services which we consume, it creates wealth and through taxation helps to pay for schools, the National Health Service and many other government and local authority services. Business also provides us with employment. It is important therefore to understand business and to appreciate how it functions in its many and varied forms to know how it affects all our lives. The aim of this chapter is to clarify the meaning and purpose of business.

1.1 Economic Activity

Business can be classified in a number of ways:

—by sector
—by level of activity
—by legal organisation and ownership.

By sector

Business activity can be divided into the *private* and *public* sectors. The private sector (private enterprise) is owned by private individuals or companies. The prime motive for such organisations is to make profit.

The public sector is that section of economic activity owned partly or wholly by the government or administered through government departments and local authorities. The objectives of such organisations vary but include the provision of services, the establishment of employment opportunities, the maintenance of law, order and defence.

4 *Business Activity*

Business activity: by sector

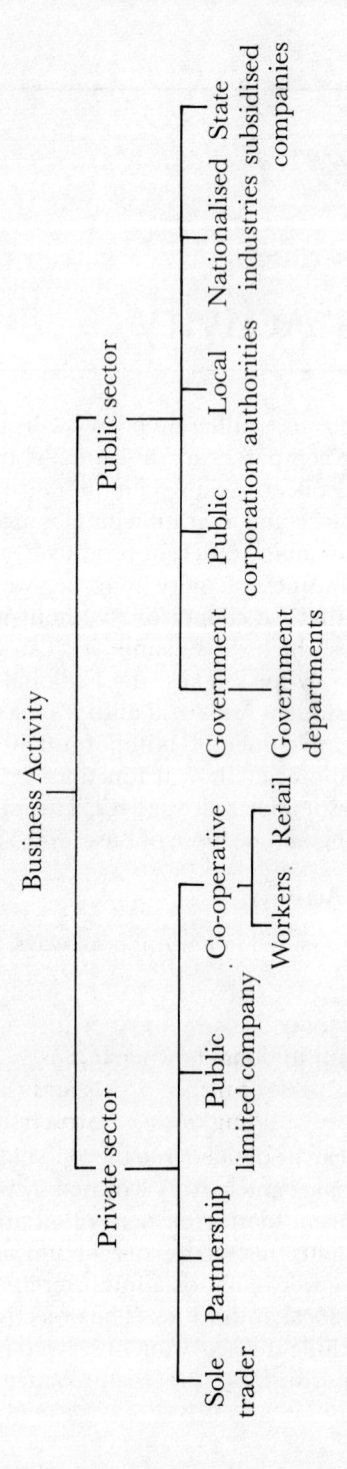

Fig. 1.1

- Business Activity
  - Private sector
    - Sole trader
    - Partnership
    - Public limited company
    - Co-operative
      - Workers
      - Retail
  - Public sector
    - Government
      - Government departments
    - Public corporation
    - Local authorities
    - Nationalised industries
    - State subsidised companies

Task

Using the diagram, see if you can identify into which sector the following organisations fall.

   (i) ICI
  (ii) British Coal
 (iii) BBC
  (iv) The Rover Group
   (v) Ford (UK)
  (vi) Local Education Authority
 (vii) British Telecom
(viii) Marks and Spencer
  (ix) British Petroleum
   (x) DHSS

By level of activity

Any product which we consume will have been involved in three distinct levels of activity, each level involving specialist businesses.

Primary activities refer to those firms involved in the first stages of production. These are extractive industries involved in extracting raw materials and food stuffs from above or below the earth's surface. They include farming, fishing, mining and oil extraction.

The primary sector employs about three per cent of the country's workforce, a figure which has remained relatively constant over the last decade.

Secondary activities are those firms involved in the secondary stage of production. They are concerned with manufacturing and construction of goods. Manufacturers will either produce a finished product or make parts or components which will be assembled by other firms to make the final product. Construction industries take raw materials and partly finished goods and change them into end products, e.g. house building, road construction.

These secondary industries employ less than thirty per cent of the workforce, although in 1976 they employed over thirty-five per cent.

This sharp decline has had a devastating effect on employment opportunities in many of the traditional United Kingdom manufacturing areas, including the North East, the North West, South Wales and the West Midlands.

Tertiary activities are the third level and relate to those firms that provide services for both the community and business. Much of the local authority spending is directed to employment in services —

social, health, education, etc. Such people are not involved directly in producing goods but in providing services for the whole of society (Direct services).

Tertiary activity also involves services to commerce (Commercial services). Trade is involved in helping goods reach the final consumer, i.e. retailing, wholesaling, importing and exporting. There are also aids to trade, which make business activity possible, such as banking, finance, insurance, transport and communications.

It is the tertiary sector which has seen the largest growth in terms of employment in the last decade, increasing by some five per cent of people employed since 1976.

Fig. 1.2

Business activity: by level of activity

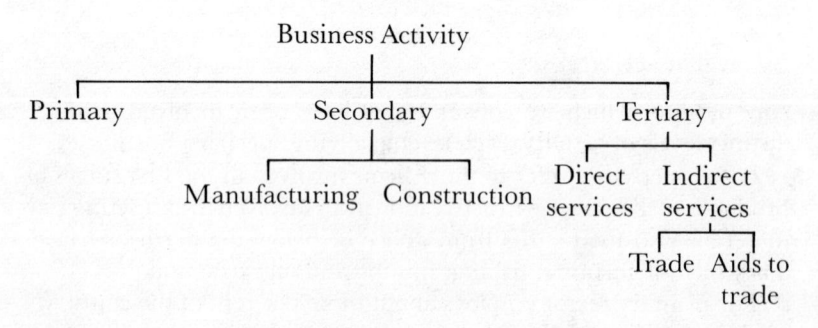

```
                    Business Activity
         ┌───────────────┼───────────────┐
      Primary        Secondary         Tertiary
                  ┌──────┴──────┐    ┌─────┴─────┐
              Manufacturing Construction Direct  Indirect
                                       services services
                                                ┌────┴────┐
                                              Trade   Aids to
                                                       trade
```

Task

Take the following jobs and place them into three lists — primary, secondary and tertiary. Then see if you can indicate which further sub-divisions they may fit into:

Farmer, teacher, builder, doctor, insurance broker, car-production worker, computer programmer, coal miner, dairy herdsman, shop worker, bank manager.

By legal organisation and ownership

Private sector firms can be legally organised in a variety of ways depending upon their size, background and financial requirements.

The smallest and newest types of business are usually formed as sole traders. The business is owned by one person, although the trader may have many employees and several branches. Any profits made go to the owner, whilst he/she will have to bear any debts from his/her personal possessions. Sole traders are the most numerous form of business organisation.

Partnerships are an extension of the sole trader, where between two and twenty people pool their finances and/or expertise. Profits are shared, losses and debts are the liability of the partners collectively. Partnerships are commonly found in building, retailing or where professional services are offered, e.g. solicitors, accountants, dentists, doctors, etc.

Joint-stock companies can be either private limited companies (Ltd.) or public limited companies. Ownership is in the form of shareholders who have a financial stake in the business by buying shares.

Private limited companies are usually small or medium sized businesses, often run and controlled by a family. Their shares are not freely available to members of the public.

The largest types of private sector organisations are the public limited companies (PLC) whose shares may be bought and sold through the market of the stock exchange. Many public limited companies have substantial investments overseas (i.e. ICI, Courtaulds, GEC) and these are known as multi-nationals. They have the same legal structure as an ordinary joint stock company, but exist in many countries simultaneously.

Sole traders, partnerships and joint stock companies attempt to maximise the profit and return of their owners' investments. Some organisations in the private sector have other motives and are known as co-operatives. The Co-operative society (Co-op) is involved in retailing and wholesaling. Any profits made are distributed to members, not in relationship to the number of shares held but in proportion to their purchases (the divi — or dividend). Like other forms of co-operatives, it is a self-help organisation, fostering the principles of members' ownership and control. In the 1970s a number of workers' co-operatives were established in an attempt to rescue ailing businesses (Triumph Motor Cycles of Meriden) and maintain employment.

Co-operatives, along with other organisations such as building societies, are often registered as Friendly Societies, whose members enjoy limited liability, whilst control and management is in the hands of full-time management committees.

Public corporations are those organisations within the public sector which have been nationalised. An enabling act either creates the corporation (e.g. 1927 — the BBC) or takes control of private enterprise already in existence (e.g. railways, coal, shipbuilding).

1.2 The Business Community

The business community plays a vital part in the economic system of the country. The business community can be seen as a network of groups of people — consumers, employees, investors, managers, all of whom perform different tasks within the economy. Yet each individual may take on several roles, showing an inter-dependence within the economy.

The consumer

The consumer is at the end of a chain of distribution and will be the final purchaser and user of a product or service.

Fig. 1.3

The chain of production/distribution

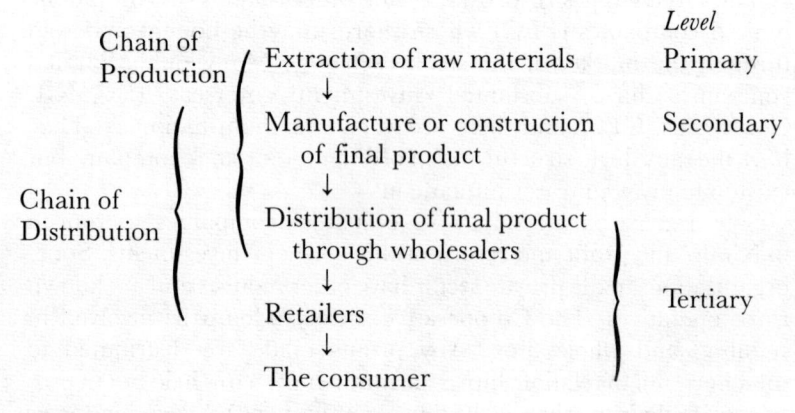

Chain	Stage	Level
Chain of Production	Extraction of raw materials	Primary
	↓	
	Manufacture or construction of final product	Secondary
	↓	
Chain of Distribution	Distribution of final product through wholesalers	
	↓	Tertiary
	Retailers	
	↓	
	The consumer	

Task

Consider an item from your breakfast (toast, tea, coffee, eggs) and identify the various stages involved in the chain of production and distribution.

From a business point of view the final consumer is of vital importance. Businesses need to know the nature and characteristics of their customers. How many people will want to buy the product, who are the main competitors, what income is available to purchase their output? These factors will influence the demand for their products or services. If a firm can measure the demand for its output, then this will determine the amount to be produced, the possible price to be charged and likely profit to be made.

Fig. 1.4

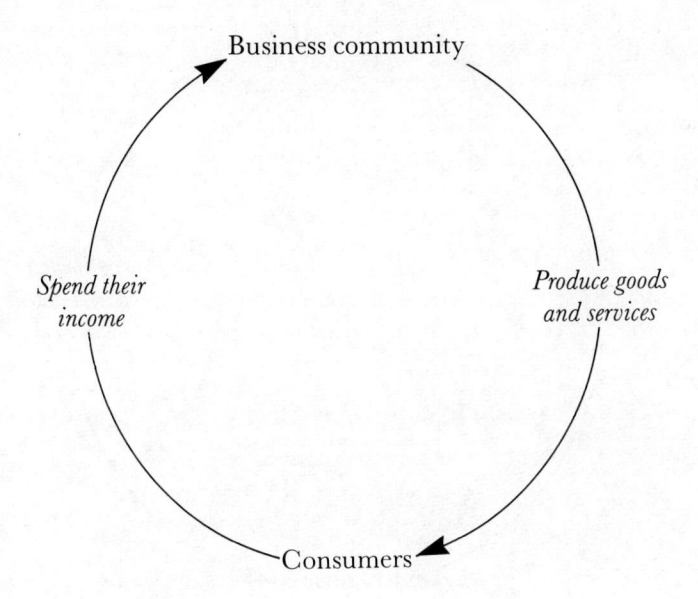

```
         Business community
        ↗                  ↘
   Spend their          Produce goods
     income             and services
        ↖                  ↙
           Consumers ←
```

The employee

In the production of goods and services, companies will need to employ people to extract, manufacture, construct and distribute their products. Employees can be classified into both their occupations and into their various economic groups.

Fig. 1.5

Example of social trend

	Male	Female
Non-Manual: employers, professional managers,	21%	5%
intermediate non-manual	18%	51%
Total non-manual	39%	56%
Manual: skilled	41%	8%
semi-skilled/unskilled	20%	36%
Total manual	61%	44%

Employees are also consumers and provide much of the income required to purchase the output of businesses.

Fig. 1.6

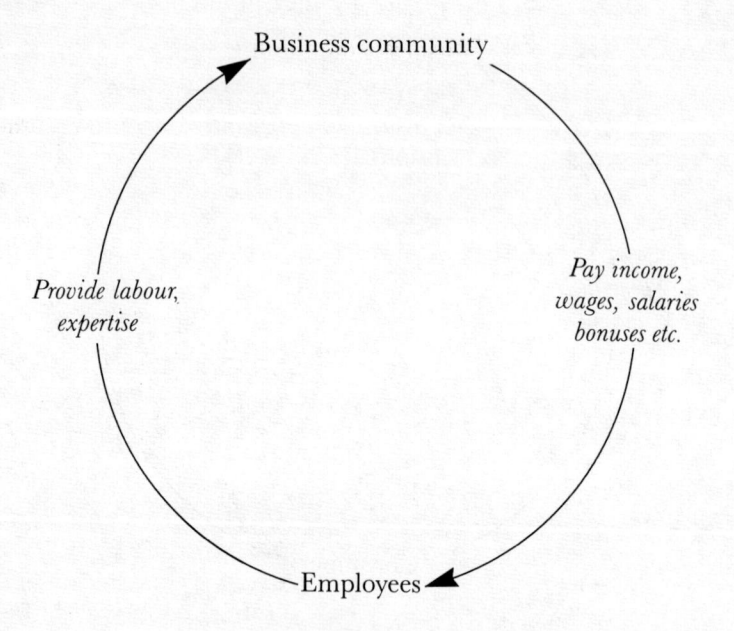

Business community

Provide labour, expertise

Pay income, wages, salaries bonuses etc.

Employees

Fig. 1.7

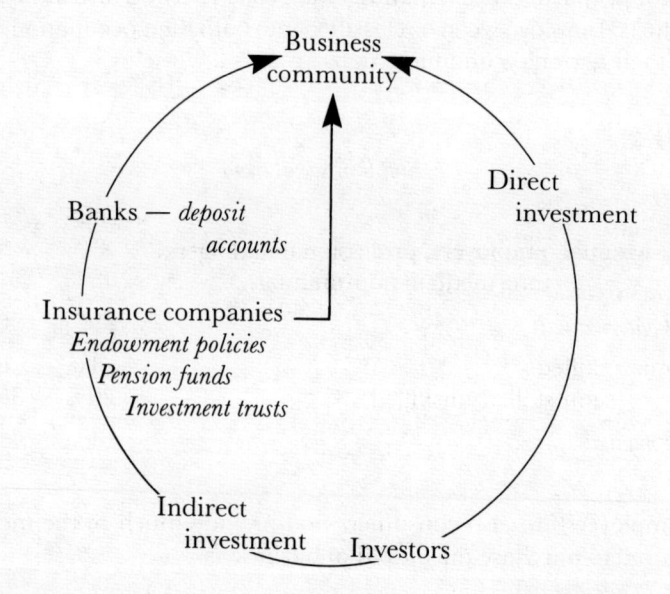

Business community

Banks — *deposit accounts*

Insurance companies
*Endowment policies
Pension funds
Investment trusts*

Direct investment

Indirect investment

Investors

Investors

Investors are members of the public who provide the finance which businesses require. Without such finance businesses would not be able to expand, develop and grow. Investors may be people who save small amounts with banks, insurance companies, investment funds, or who contribute to pension funds. Such savings are indirect investments, their funds will often find their way through financial institutions into companies (often through the Stock Exchange). Other investors will place their money directly with companies either as shareholders or as partners.

Managers

Managers are specialist employees engaged by businesses to run companies and organisations. The manager may also be the owner as in smaller types of business organisations such as sole traders and partnerships. More often managers may control the daily activities of a business and are responsible to the owners (shareholders) through a board of directors (who themselves are senior managers). This division between owners and professional managers is known as the divorcing of management and ownership and is a common feature of modern industrial society.

Fig. 1.8

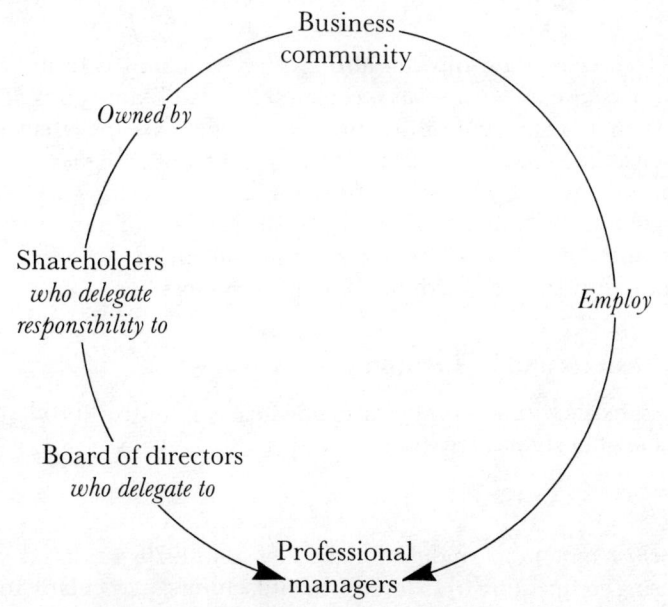

Business community
Owned by
Shareholders
who delegate responsibility to
Employ
Board of directors
who delegate to
Professional managers

It can be seen that consumers, employees, investors and managers are necessary people who perform tasks which are all vital to the business community and are inter-linked. Thus a person at any one time may be a consumer as well as an employee, also an investor and perhaps a manager.

Fig. 1.9

The inter-relationship of the business community

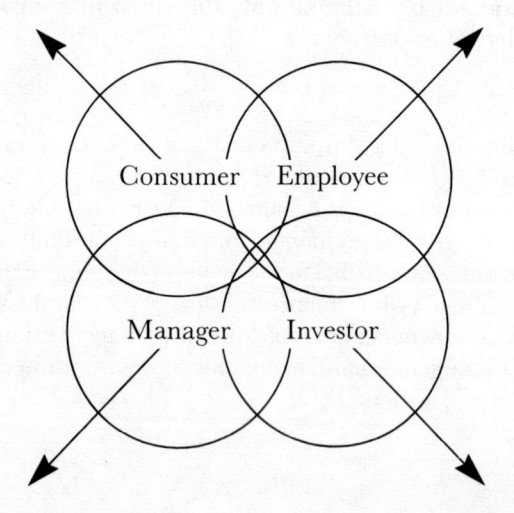

Such inter-relationship can also give rise to conflicts of interest, thus a person may wish — as a consumer — to obtain goods of the highest quality and at the lowest price; as an employee they may wish to receive the highest pay, as an investor to obtain the highest return of their money and as a manager to gain the highest efficiency. Such separate interests are all pulling the business community in various conflicting directions and may result in antagonism (e.g. industrial action, redundancies or exploitation of consumers).

1.3 Business and its Environment

Business exists within an environment which will control and change the value of business activity.

Example

The British motor cycle industry in the 1960s and 1970s was faced with increasing competition from foreign manufacturers, particularly from the Japanese, whose motor cycles were imported into this country. These were technologically advanced and considerably cheaper than British motor cycles. Very quickly the United Kingdom industry went into decline. BSA, the largest concern, faced collapse and bankruptcy. In March 1973 the government decided to act to preserve the industry. Large sums of money were pumped into the company (£4.8 millions), and at the same time the industry was restructured to include an amalgamation with another firm, Norton-Villiers.

The reconstruction of the industry in the long run was to fail. The example shows how outside pressures of both economic events (external competition) and government action shaped and influenced an industry. Such action as this is constantly affecting businesses of all sizes and within all markets. In particular the government has a substantial effect on business.

The role of government and business

We have already noted how the government owns and directly controls a large part of economic activity. Such control is through the ownership of public corporations and nationalised industries as well as through the spending of huge amounts of money by government departments and local authorities.

All businesses in whichever country they exist have some control exerted by central government. What varies between countries is the amount and degree of such control. In the United Kingdom we have an economy which is a mixture of both private and public sectors. Such a mixture will vary according to the political persuasion of the government of the day. Thus the United Kingdom economy fluctuates from more state control and nationalisation to less government intervention and a greater degree of privatisation. All other economies also experience such movement although they may have different starting points.

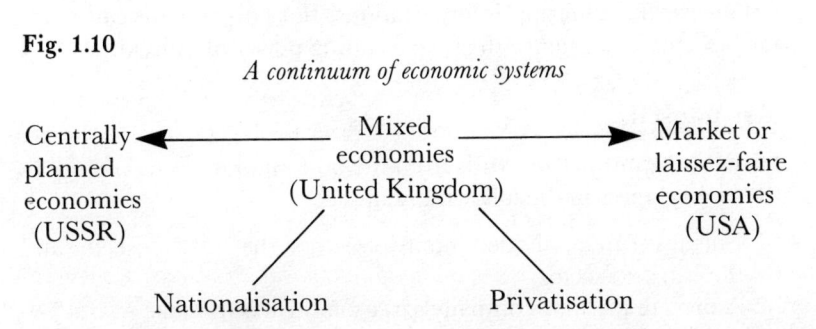

Fig. 1.10

A continuum of economic systems

Centrally planned economies (USSR) ←——— Mixed economies (United Kingdom) ———→ Market or laissez-faire economies (USA)

Nationalisation   Privatisation

No economic system has a total control by a central government, or a complete lack of central government control. However, the USSR has a largely centrally-controlled system, where five-year plans indicate the type and scale of output of the business community. The United States of America on the other hand has a small public sector, where output is determined by the wishes of consumers and the output of producers (the market). The government deliberately avoids controlling or regulating business activity except where it is required to do so in the interest of the consumer.

The United Kingdom business community fits between these two extreme forms of economic system. In our mixed economic system the government plays an active role exerting pressures on both producers and consumers. It is possible to see a number of areas where government intervention is seen as necessary on behalf of the community as a whole.

(a) *National responsibility* — the government has national responsibility for both security (armed forces) and national welfare (health, education, social security). Governments may try to manipulate the economy to reduce unemployment, to control inflation, to encourage national output to grow, to influence foreign trade. Such responsibilities will have a substantial effect on consumers, employees, investors and managers through the taxation policy and spending programmes (fiscal policy).

(b) *Government ownership* — the government directly owns 40 per cent of all business undertakings within the public sector. Such ownership may be due to the government's wish to control certain industries which may be best organised as a monopoly (i.e. only one organisation controlling an entire industry) e.g. electricity, rail, coal, steel. This ensures that prices and output of such industries are influenced by and ultimately responsible to government and its elected representatives.

(c) *Reduce unfairness* — in particular the tax system, which can be used to reduce inequalities in people's income and wealth. The idea of unfairness has differing interpretations, but government can make judgements to influence the real spending power of individuals.

Test Yourself

Using the appropriate words from the bottom of this exercise, fill in the blank spaces in the following sentences:

1 Business can be divided into two sectors, the . . . . . . sector and the . . . . . . sector.
2 A private . . . . . . company's main motive is to make . . . . . .

3 There are three levels of business activities. These are ......, ... and ......
4 An insurance company is an example of a ......
5 The smallest type of businesses are usually organised as ......
6 The ...... is the last link in the chain of distribution.
7 People who provide finance for businesses are called ......
8 The USSR is an example of a ......
9 The UK is described as a ......
10 Moving a firm or industry from the public sector to the private sector is called ......

tertiary   sector   privatisation   secondary   consumer

investors   public   commercial service   profit   primary

private   centrally planned economy   mixed economy

sole traders

Chapter 2
Business Structure and Organisation

In Britain business activity is carried on either within the private sector or the public sector. It is this combination which gives us the description of a mixed economy. The degree of mixture depends upon the preferences and political persuasion of the government at the time.

In this chapter we shall examine the types of business organisations which exist in the private sector of the British economy. It will be apparent that the type of legal arrangements appropriate to a small one-man business, such as a decorator, will be inappropriate to large multi-nationals like ICI or GEC. For this reason businesses in the private sector can be divided into five distinct kinds, each appropriate to a type and size of business. These are:

The sole trader
Partnerships
Private limited companies (Ltd)
Public limited companies (PLC)
Co-operatives.

2.1 The Sole Trader

The most important feature of this type of business is that it is a small business owned by one person. Often several people are employed and they may work from a number of different premises. Most new businesses begin as sole traders, as the office work involved is minimal and there are few legal restrictions and regulations. Gardeners, decorators, plumbers, small retailers, removal firms, small factories and indeed business in most fields may be owned by sole traders.

The advantages of being a sole trader may be listed as follows:

(i) All the profit goes to the owner.
(ii) All decisions are in the hands of the owner.
(iii) The owner can have personal contact with all of the business, its employees and its customers.

(iv) The owner does not need large amounts of money to start up the business.
(v) Sole traders often gain direct financial returns for their hard work.

Such advantages are often the stimulus for people to go into business on their own.

Case Examples

(a) June Smith had worked in a clothes shop for ten years and she had built up considerable experience. On the death of her parents she inherited some money and decided to open up her own shop. At last she was her own boss, able to keep all the profits.

(b) Matthew Brown was an excellent mechanic but the garage where he worked went out of business. He received a small redundancy settlement and using a government grant, he set up his own workshop repairing and renovating second-hand cars.

(c) Jim Green had worked for the same large building company for thirty years. He was tired of being told what to do and how to do it. By using his own savings he bought an old van and started advertising in the local paper. He is now running his own building firm and employing three other people.

(d) Trevor Winter was a local athlete of some repute. He decided to give up his job as a lecturer at the Technical College and, using the basement at his home, set up a fitness centre. His many friends and contacts in the sporting circles became his first clients.

Whilst these examples are of successful ventures as sole traders, there are tens of thousands of businesses that fail each year, the majority of which are also sole traders. Such businesses usually lack experience and are open to pressures from larger and more established businesses. Often their owners attempt to grow too quickly and overstretch their resources. Alternatively they may make unrealistic estimates as to the size and scale of the market they are entering.

One of the major problems facing a sole trader is that they are personally responsible for all the debts incurred by their business. This is known as *unlimited liability*. Any sole trader who cannot meet his debts may be taken to the bankruptcy court. The court will calculate how much the person owes and take such money from his own assets as well as those of the business. This may include his house, car, furniture, etc. As the business in the eyes of the law is the person (i.e.

the business has no legal identity) this may mean that everything he owns has to be sold, leaving only the tools of his trade and £20 of bedding and clothes. At this point the person will be declared bankrupt and will not be allowed to obtain credit above £10 without admitting this. Only when all the previous debts are cleared will the person be discharged by the courts.

Other disadvantages to being a sole trader are:

(a) Difficulty in raising capital to start up the business. Banks are often reluctant to provide loans or extend overdraft facilities to small, new, sole trading businesses. The high degree of risk, the lack of expertise and security often put off the traditional business investor. (N.B. The government under the loans guarantee scheme has often underwritten bank loans to small investors. Small businesses can also use incentive schemes provided by local authorities or the manpower services commission to provide cash or take on workers at a considerable subsidy.)

(b) Difficulty in obtaining credit arrangements from suppliers, which often means cash payment for items prior to delivery. Such a handicap will often tie up valuable cash and create cash-flow or liquidity problems for the business. Suppliers themselves will often be reluctant to give credit facilities, due to uncertainty of the small business. Also such customers are by nature usually only requiring low volume orders and so have little power in determining preferential arrangements with their suppliers.

If the owner falls ill or cannot trade for any reason, then the business will quickly fail. Often the owner is the business.

2.2 Partnerships

Often a sole trader, lacking money or expertise, may seek a partner to expand and stabilise the business. The 1890 Partnership Act allows this type of business to have between two and twenty persons as members. There are exceptions, such as banks who are not allowed to have more than ten partners and certain professional firms such as accountants, solicitors and stockbrokers who are allowed more than twenty partners.

Jim Green, the builder, found that after trading on his own account for eighteen months the work was becoming too much for him. His son, Alf, had served an apprenticeship as a carpenter but was now unemployed. At his father's suggestion Alf went into business with him; he had some of his own savings to help to buy a newer van. More important was the fact that Jim no longer had to sub-contract any carpentry work out to another firm. Jim Green, Builder, now became Jim Green & Son, Builders and Carpenters, and the type of work that they could take on increased accordingly. Jim hoped that eventually he could retire from the business leaving the firm and its reputation in Alf's hands. At this point Jim would be a *dormant* or *sleeping partner*, i.e. keeping his investment in the business and so sharing in any profits made but not taking an active part in its running.

Just like a sole trader, partnerships have unlimited liability but in this case each partner is equally liable for any debts incurred by the business. To safeguard the interests of the partners, it is usual for partnerships to draw up a Deed of Partnership. This legal document outlines the rights and duties of each partner. It may detail how profits are to be shared, what happens upon the death or retirement of a partner, how decisions are to be made and what happens if the partnership gets into financial difficulties. Without such a Deed it is assumed that responsibility for the partnership is shared equally amongst all the partners. It will also be assumed, according to the Partnership Act, that all profits will be divided equally amongst the partners irrespective of their investment in the business.

Some people may be reluctant to invest in a partnership because of the risks of unlimited liability. Thus within the Deed of Partnership it is possible for some partners to be *limited partners*, i.e. their liability ends with the amount of money put into the business, safeguarding their own possessions. In any partnership there must be one active partner with unlimited liability.

Limited liability

Partnerships and sole traders are obviously not suited for the development of large businesses. The reasons for this are threefold:

(i) The amount of money needed must come from a far larger number of people.
(ii) The fear of unlimited liability will not encourage outsiders to invest in the business.
(iii) Upon the death of the owner or a partner, the business ceases to exist and this will deter continual expansion and growth.

For these reasons, various Acts of Parliament allow for the formation of limited liability companies (or joint stock companies).

The money or capital required for these businesses is divided into shares which can be sold to members of the public. Such investors are known as shareholders and become collectively the owners of the business. If the business were to fail then the shareholders would only lose the money they had paid in for their shares and nothing more. Thus their liability is limited to their investment.

There are two distinct types of limited company: private limited companies and public limited companies which are registered as an artificial 'person'. This means that in the eyes of the law they have a separate legal identity. They can conduct business, employ people, make contracts, be responsible for debts and be sued in their own name. This is different from sole traders and partnerships who have no such distinction in law — the business in their case is the owner who is personally responsible for all trading activities that go on in his company.

2.3 Private Limited Companies (Ltd)

These businesses are usually of a medium size, often owned and controlled by a family. They are private in the sense that shares can only be sold privately and with the agreement of the other shareholders. Such businesses must have at least two shareholders and private companies cannot sell their shares through the Stock Exchange nor advertise their shares publicly.

As share ownership is very restricted in a private company, long-term expansion is often limited to the retained profits made by the business. Often, such growth may limit trading activity and private companies often seek either a stock exchange flotation and/or approval to register as a public company.

2.4 Public Limited Companies (PLC)

These are the largest companies in the country, many of them being household names (ICI, Marks & Spencer, Boots, GEC, etc.). These companies must have a minimum of two shareholders and there is no maximum. They are allowed to sell their shares to the public and transfer of shares is simple, therefore the number of owners can be considerable.

Obviously for all the shareholders to take part in the running of the business would not be practical, and so as with smaller Private Limited Companies they elect a board of directors who are responsible for the daily conduct and management of the business. Such an arrangement is known as the separation (or divorcing) of ownership from control. It allows the shareholders to maintain overall control while delegating the business affairs of the company to a group of specialist managers. This board is then answerable to the owners through the voting rights which share-ownership gives. If a substantial number of shareholders were disappointed with the running or performance of the business then they could collectively vote against the directors at the annual general meeting (AGM) of the company.

The AGM is called once a year and is an invitation to all shareholders to hear the policies of the company. In advance of the meeting the shareholders will receive a copy of the Chairman's Report. This outlines the overall strategy and attempts to explain the company's performance. Following this report are the annual accounts of the business which must include a copy of the Balance Sheet and Profit and Loss Account (see Chapter 7). These give information about the financial state of the company and its profitability. These accounts have to be audited or certified as correct by an outside firm of accountants. A distribution of profits to shareholders will be recommended in the form of a dividend, the remaining profits being kept for future expansion.

Shareholders at the AGM will be allowed to put questions to any member of the Board and then vote on whether to accept the report, its accounts and the proposed dividend. The power of any one shareholder is limited to the proportion of shares held. Thus the controlling influence is often in the hands of the largest shareholders. Indeed, many small shareholders do not even attend the AGM.

Fig. 2.1

The separation of ownership from control

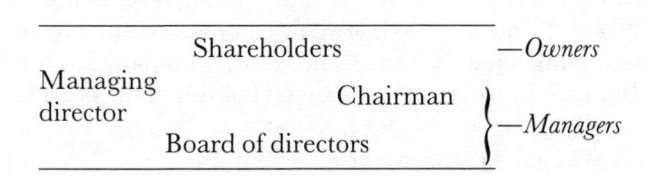

Shareholders	—Owners
Managing director Chairman Board of directors	—Managers

The details of purchasing shares and the mechanics of raising capital through the Stock Exchange is covered in depth in Chapter 6.

2.5 Co-operatives

The Co-operative movement began as a formal method of trading in 1844 in Rochdale (though co-operatives had existed long before this). A group of industrial workers decided to set up their own shop in competition with local traders who they felt were offering over-priced and poor quality products. The principles of the Rochdale Pioneers still exist today, whereby anyone can become a member of the Co-operative Society. A dividend is paid out to members according to the amount purchased. This 'divi' can be taken in cash or as a discount on future purchases. Today trading stamps are given in Co-op shops, with members gaining the advantage of higher values for a book of stamps than non-members, when the book is paid into their share account.

Membership costs a small fee and each member has equal voting rights irrespective of the amount they have invested in the Society.

The Society is involved in activities outside of retailing and wholesaling, such as education and politics.

Societies are organised on an area basis to avoid competing against each other. Each society is usually based around a central department store selling a wide range of products, with satellite shops and supermarkets scattered around the area. Societies will often also run wholesalers, dairies, milk-rounds, bakeries and undertaking services. Recently the Co-op has moved most successfully into the high street banking sector, offering a wide range of financial services to its members.

The basis of self-help stimulated by the retail co-ops has been mirrored in the development of worker co-operatives. Often these have been set up out of an ailing company — the workers have organised themselves to raise the funds needed to purchase the assets of the business. Then collective workers' committees have been formed to control, manage and organise the company, setting it on a new footing. The motivation for success has come from the hands of the workers who see that they have a financial as well as a managerial stake in the business. While many co-operatives of this type have been successful, a number have failed as the company has been unable to eliminate the original commercial failures of the previous business.

2.6 Legal Arrangements

Various Acts of Parliament are presently in force which are designed to control the trading activities of companies. Such control is to provide protection for shareholders, consumers and employees, against over-zealous business practices.

Company registration

In Britain companies are formed in accordance with Acts of

Parliament called The Companies' Acts, the most recent being in 1976, 1980 and 1981. These Acts dictate that when a company is formed a solicitor draws up two documents, the Memorandum of Association and the Articles of Association. These two documents must be sent to the Registrar of Companies by the promoters of the business.

The Memorandum of Association

The Memorandum of Association consists of six main clauses:

(i) Name clause states the name of the business and will indicate its status by the letters PLC for Public Limited Company and Ltd for a private limited company.

(ii) Situation Clause indicates the country where the company is officially registered, i.e. the registered office.

(iii) Objects clause states the object for which the company is established, e.g. to carry out plumbing work in domestic households.

(iv) Liability clause states what the liability of investors is; this is usually limited.

(v) Capital clause states the amount of capital with which the company is to be registered and the way in which it is to be divided into shares, for example £500000 divided into 50p shares. Any public company must have a nominal share capital of at least £50000.

(vi) Association clause declares that the signatories (minimum of two) wish to form the company and pay for the number of shares shown.

Articles of Association

This document outlines the internal relationship of the company and must bear the same signatures as the Memorandum of Association.

Included in the 'Articles' will be the rights of shareholders, the arrangements for calling annual general meetings and extraordinary general meetings, the methods of electing directors and the division of profits. Such details can be readily altered by the shareholders if they wish, providing such alterations do not conflict with the memorandum of association.

Before formal registration of a company the promoters will also have to provide the Registrar of Companies with:

(i) A declaration made under oath through a solicitor that all requirements of the various Companies' Acts will be met.

(ii) A list of first directors.
(iii) Address of registered office.
(iv) Statement of consent written by each proposed director confirming that they are willing to act in this capacity.

Accounts

All companies are required by the Companies' Act to supply certain information annually to the Department of Trade. They must give details of shareholders, the directors and the company's assets, along with the Balance Sheet and Profit and Loss Account of the company.

As mentioned earlier in this chapter, both the Balance Sheet and Profit and Loss Account will need to be checked or audited by a qualified firm of accountants. In this way, owners, workers, customers, suppliers and even the tax collectors of the Inland Revenue will be assured that an independent specialist has examined the trading records of the company and that such records are 'a true and fair view of the company'.

Test Yourself

Using the appropriate words from the bottom of this exercise, fill in the blank spaces in the following sentences:

1. Small businesses owned by one person are called ......
2. Sole traders and partnerships have ......
3. If a person contributes capital to a partnership but is not involved in its daily running he/she is called ......
4. The initials PLC stand for ......
5. Separating ...... from ...... is a common feature of PLC's.
6. Shareholders are invited to an ......
7. The ...... were the originators of the retail co-op.
8. The ...... specifies the external relationship of a business.
9. The Companies' Acts require all companies to produce a set of ......
10. ...... will check that the accounts of a business give a 'true and fair view'.

sleeping partner   managers   Rochdale Pioneers

annual general meeting   auditors   unlimited liability

accounts   sole traders   owners

Memorandum of Association   Public Limited Company

Questions

1. What are the main types of business organisations found in the private sector?
2. What are the advantages of a sole trader taking on a partner?
3. Distinguish between unlimited and limited liability.
4. What safeguards does the shareholder have when investing in a public limited company?
5. What is the separation of ownership from control? Why is it a feature of most large companies?
6. Why do differing legal arrangements allow a variety of business organisations to exist in the United Kingdom?

Chapter 3

Internal Organisation

There is no such thing as a typical company, but in this chapter we shall outline in general the type of organisation that might exist within a medium- to large-sized manufacturing company. Later in the chapter we shall examine the issues which face the internal organisation of any business.

3.1 The Structure of a Company

All organisations have some form of internal structure. If you consider a school, college or club they all have some form of leadership and a degree of delegation. This is the same within business (except for the smallest one-person concern).

Fig. 3.1 *The structure of a company*

The structure of a medium-sized manufacturing company may be similar to that given below:

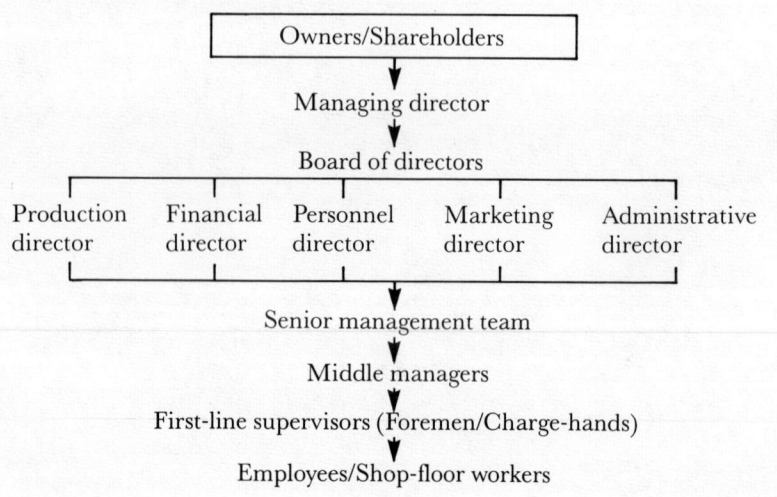

```
                    Owners/Shareholders
                            ↓
                    Managing director
                            ↓
                    Board of directors
    ┌───────────┬───────────┬───────────┬───────────┬───────────┐
 Production  Financial  Personnel   Marketing  Administrative
 director    director   director    director    director
    └───────────┴───────────┴─────┬─────┴───────────┴───────────┘
                                  ↓
                    Senior management team
                            ↓
                     Middle managers
                            ↓
        First-line supervisors (Foremen/Charge-hands)
                            ↓
               Employees/Shop-floor workers
```

Task

Draw up a chart, similar to the one above, for an organisation with which you are familiar, other than a business, e.g. a school/college/club, etc.

Each of the directors in the diagram will be responsible for a specialist department. That department will consist of a group of people who are under the overall control of the director. Each director will have the responsibility of turning the Board of directors' policies into the practical daily applications of his department. He will have a cost budget with which to work and a series of specific objectives to fulfil. Thus the production director may have a budget of £500 000 to cover all costs involved in producing the product, including labour, overtime, department administration, raw material components, etc. Within this quota he may be expected to produce so many tons of output, or 'x' number of parts, or generate £1 000 000 of produced units. Within this framework the director is given a wide range of freedom in pursuing these objectives, answerable and accountable to other directors and to the company's shareholders.

If we examine each department in turn we can identify the main areas of responsibility and activity in a company.

3.2 The Production Department

The production department and its director are responsible for converting component and raw materials into finished products. Often the production department will employ the bulk of the labour force. Within the department may be the following structure:

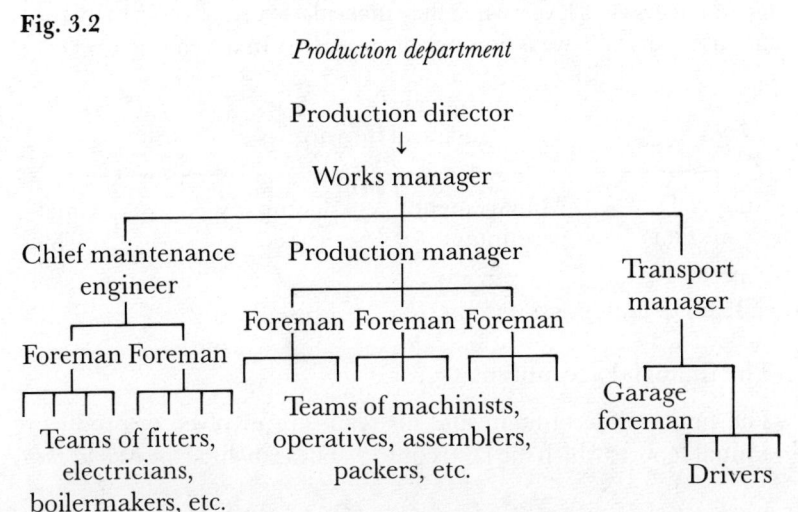

Fig. 3.2

Production department

```
                        Production director
                                ↓
                         Works manager
         ┌──────────────────────┼──────────────────────┐
  Chief maintenance      Production manager      Transport
      engineer                                    manager
         │              ┌───────┼───────┐            │
   Foreman Foreman   Foreman Foreman Foreman    Garage
     │       │         │       │       │        foreman
  ┌┬┬┐    ┌┬┬┐      ┌┬┬┐    ┌┬┬┐    ┌┬┬┐         │
  Teams of fitters,   Teams of machinists,     ┌─┴─┐
    electricians,    operatives, assemblers,   Drivers
  boilermakers, etc.    packers, etc.
```

The main job of the department is to produce goods to agreed targets, to ensure that quality of output is maintained to a level acceptable to the customer, to control costs, or minimise wastage, to maintain machinery and install new equipment when required. To perform so many tasks, the department relies on the work of other departments. Thus the marketing department will give information about customer requirements (e.g. delivery dates, standard of finish, etc.). The personnel department will ensure that the manpower needs of the factory are met. The finance department will provide data concerning the costs of the department.

As the department employs such a large number of people, much of the work of the management will be in dealing with people. Production managers will need to motivate their workforce and provide an effective working environment in which their employees can operate. In many modern factories the production process has been progressively automated. At the same time attempts have been made to improve working conditions by reducing noise levels, heat, dirt and other similar problems.

3.3 The Finance Department

The finance department is under the management of the financial director who is in control of the information relating to the money involved in the business. The department has to know when and how much money is coming into and going out of the business. It also needs to know the sources of such finance.

The financial director must have at hand the exact monetary position of the business at any time. Such information will be required by managers at all levels when they make decisions. To help in this task the director will have a number of specialists in his charge.

Fig. 3.3

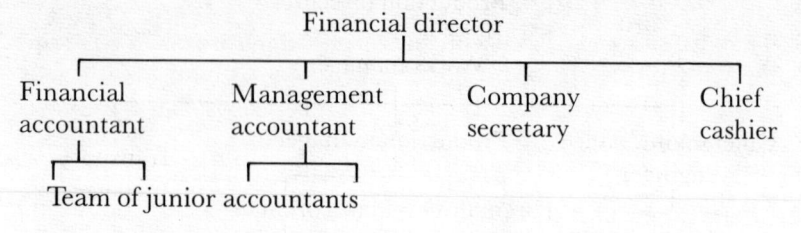

```
                        Financial director
         ┌──────────────┬─────────────┬──────────────┐
    Financial       Management      Company         Chief
    accountant      accountant      secretary       cashier
    ┌────┐          ┌────┐
    Team of junior accountants
```

The financial accountant

The financial accountant and his team are involved in producing annual reports which the law requires. These include the *balance sheet*, *profit and loss account* (see Chapter 7) and *cash flow forecasts*. Such information may also be prepared on a more regular basis for use by managers. The financial section will also deal with the payment of day-to-day transactions such as wages and invoices from suppliers.

The management accountant

The management accountant provides more detailed information than that given in the financial statements. He will draw up specific budgets for departments, in consultation with those people responsible for the budgets. These accountants are involved in the detailed daily performance of the whole business. The information they provide helps managers and supervisors to control their sections and aids decision-making.

Task

Imagine you are the foreman of a section in the production department, responsible for eight operatives. What information do you think you and the management accountant may discuss?

The company secretary

The company secretary deals with the firm's legal position. As more laws have been passed affecting the running of companies (various Companies' Acts, the annual Finance Act, health and safety regulations, consumer legislation, equal opportunities and Industrial Relations Law), firms need experts in these matters. Small firms will use their accountants for such matters and employ specialist solicitors when complicated legal problems arise. Larger firms will have their own company secretariat.

The chief cashier

The chief cashier will deal with the daily handling of money, including the banking of cheques and money and the management of petty cash. The chief cashier may also be involved in the long-term planning of the financial requirements of the business.

3.4 The Personnel Department

The personnel department under its director or manager is concerned with the selection, recruitment and training of people within the firm. The department will be directly involved in the industrial/labour relations within the business. Any issue concerning the welfare of the company's employees will also concern the department. The department handles all those aspects of the firm concerning the people employed within the company.

The structure of the department may be:

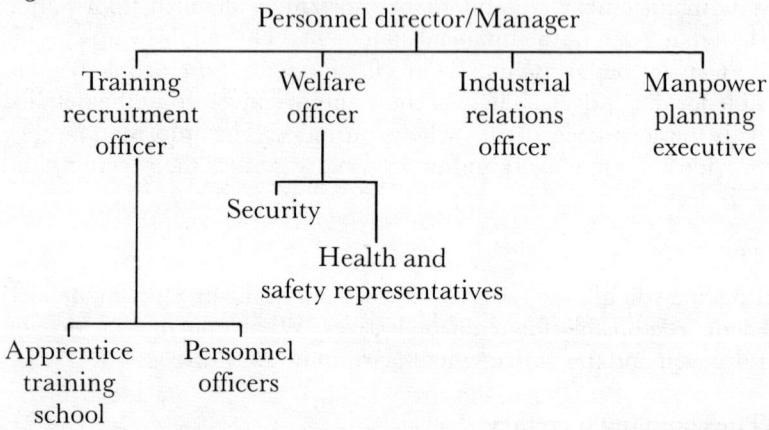

Fig. 3.4

```
                    Personnel director/Manager
        ┌──────────────┬──────────────┬──────────────┐
   Training         Welfare       Industrial      Manpower
  recruitment       officer        relations      planning
    officer                         officer       executive
                       │
                   Security
                       │
                 Health and
             safety representatives
        ┌──────────┐
   Apprentice   Personnel
    training    officers
     school
```

The recruitment officer

When a job vacancy arises the recruitment officer will consult the section concerned and handle the administration of a new appointment. This will involve drafting and placing an advertisement, selecting appropriate candidates for interviewing, administering the interview arrangements and organising the induction of the new member of staff. Training of employees may involve Youth Training Scheme trainees or apprentices. Increasingly the personnel department is involved in retraining employees to new working methods and in using different equipment.

The welfare officer

The welfare officer is concerned with any social problems a worker may experience both within the firm or outside. Through counselling interviews the officer may be able to help with absenteeism, lateness, medical problems, family circumstances, etc. Such concern is in the interest of both the employee and of the company.

Industrial relations

The industrial relations aspect of the department covers the negotiations with trade unions or worker representatives. This is a specialist task involving expertise in discussion, persuasion, industrial law, as well as providing advice to supervisors on whose shoulders responsibility for employee relations ultimately rests.

Manpower planning executive

Within the company, management will want to ensure that the right people fill the right jobs. This task lies with the manpower planning executive. The job involves forecasting future needs — and matching these requirements with the appropriate personnel. The executive may run courses to develop management skills within their own personnel.

3.5 The Marketing Department

The marketing department under the director establishes what the customer requires. The department then tries to ensure that the customer gets the goods and services at the price they have agreed, at the time specified, in the quantities required and at a quality which is acceptable.

The department covers many diverse functions:

Fig. 3.5

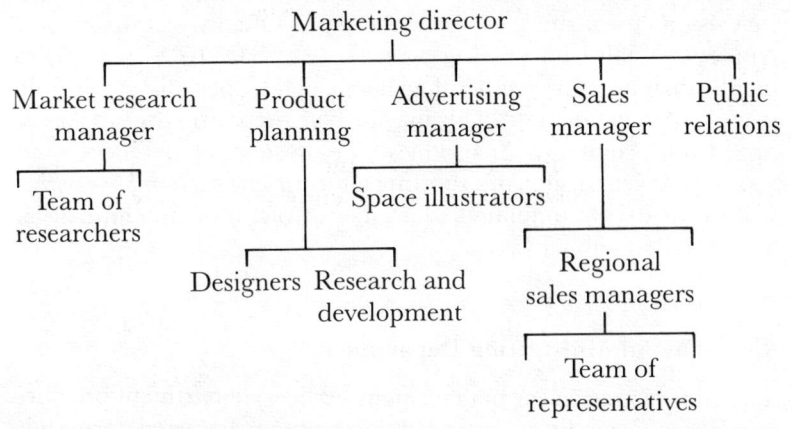

```
                        Marketing director
      ┌──────────────┬──────────┬──────────┬──────────┐
Market research   Product   Advertising   Sales      Public
   manager       planning    manager     manager    relations
      │             │           │           │
 ┌────┴────┐        │    Space illustrators  │
 Team of             │                       │
researchers          │                  ┌────┴─────┐
                ┌────┴─────┐            Regional
              Designers  Research and   sales managers
                        development          │
                                       ┌─────┴─────┐
                                         Team of
                                      representatives
```

The market research team

The market research team will provide information about the type of market the product is in. The number of potential customers, the likely pricing of the goods, and the competition which exists are all areas of interest to this section. This research may be from secondary sources — e.g. government statistics, industrial journals, etc. — when it is known as desk research. It may also involve primary research, using teams of market researchers and questionnaires. Specialist firms of market researchers may carry out such work for the company. Such information is invaluable, and often provides the starting-point for a new product — its design, packaging and advertising (see Chapter 4).

Product planning

Product planning will work closely with the production department, in designing the new product or improving an existing one. It will examine the costs of production and provide useful information to the management accountants. The department will also be researching new products (research and development department) to translate consumer demands into reality.

The advertising manager

The advertising manager is responsible for ensuring that the potential customer is aware of the product and its advantages over competitors' products. This often involves communication through the media (television, magazines, newspapers, etc.). Often a company may employ specialist advertising agencies (e.g. Saatchi & Saatchi) to handle their accounts, rather than have a highly specialist staff whose work load may fluctuate. This may involve preparing press releases, producing company magazines, organising conferences and sponsored events (often of a sporting nature). The *public relations officer* will also deal with complaints which may involve the company in legal action or bad publicity.

3.6 The Administration Department

The administration (or management services) department provides much of the back-up to the rest of the company. In overall terms it is concerned with the efficiency of the company, the flow of information, the organisation of work and the decision-making. It consists of the following specialist areas:

Fig. 3.6

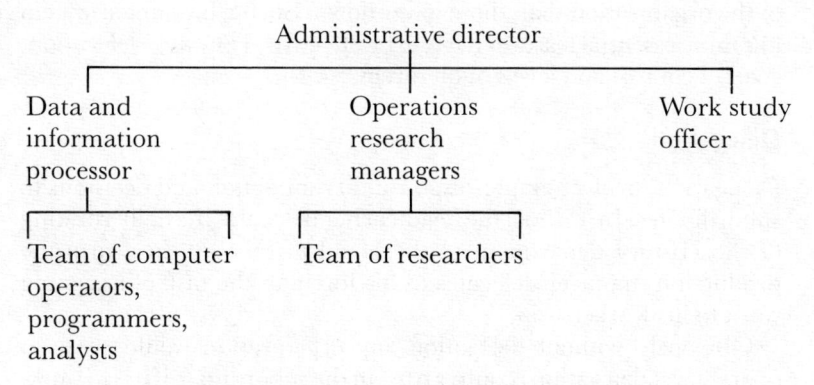

```
                    Administrative director
        ┌───────────────────┼───────────────────┐
   Data and            Operations           Work study
   information         research             officer
   processor           managers
        │                   │
   ┌────┴────┐         ┌────┴────┐
   Team of computer    Team of researchers
   operators,
   programmers,
   analysts
```

All companies need information to make decisions. Such information may be financial or concern marketing and production data. Computers can process and analyse information quickly and efficiently. Managers and decision-makers at all levels need such information. The data/information processor's job, along with his team, is to design systems and computer programs which aid this information stream thus ensuring that all who need information have it in such a form that they can interpret and analyse it. This section of most business has expanded rapidly in the past decade and it may be expected that such developments will continue. Large companies may use main frame computers, or employ agencies such as IBM or ICL to carry out such work. Small firms may use micro computers, word processors, computer networks, etc., to aid this essential flow of information.

The *operations research team* examines production methods, stock control, company documentation (invoices, statements, etc.), office lay-out and routine. It is their task to improve working methods and so reduce costs and maximise efficiency.

Within the production department, work-study engineers will have similar aims. Using method study and work measurement (see Chapter 9), such engineers will measure work methods and identify weakness and areas for improvement. It is an area which requires both technical skill and considerable diplomacy.

3.7 Control

We have seen how within any organisation there exists a formal structure. Within such a structure a hierarchy of responsibility exists, with those at the top having greater control and influence on the affairs of the organisation than those lower down. Such a hierarchal system has three essential features if it is to be effective. They are: delegation, span of control and levels of hierarchy.

Delegation

Delegation involves giving responsibility for action and decisions to subordinates. In a school the headteacher delegates the daily running of the History department to the Head of History. In a firm the production manager delegates to his foreman the task of assigning work to his workers.

Obviously without delegation any organisation would cease to operate, yet delegation requires trust in the subordinate if it is to work. Only when the manager feels that he can trust an individual with a task will delegation occur. Trust involves risk because the superior is still held accountable for things that others have done. However, providing that the manager has confidence in his subordinate's ability, delegation can take place. Such delegation then allows specialisation to take place, as the individual performs the tasks expected and eventually becomes an expert in his particular area.

Task

Consider a task you have been given to do regularly, e.g. mowing lawns, walking the dog, collecting the petty cash from the bank. Now ask yourself the following questions:

1. Who did the task prior to you?
2. Why were you given the task?
3. Do you now perform the task well?
4. Who is responsible for the job being done?

Span of control

Span of control or span of management is the number of people who are directly responsible to any one manager. Research in Ohio, USA, has shown that span of control is often related to the size of the organisation. A business of around 100 employees had managers who had four or five people responsible and reportable to them, whereas larger concerns with over 3000 employees would have spans of nine or ten people. The size of the span can be as large as thirty people depending on the nature of the organisation. The ideal span, however, would seem to depend upon the following points:

(i) The better trained the subordinate the less support is required by the manager.
(ii) The clearer the task delegated and the wider the authority given for carrying them out the less the need to refer action to a superior.
(iii) If a person is controlling a group of people all with relatively similar duties, then he may clearly look after more people than if each person had a completely unique field of activity.
(iv) If the organisation is stable with change occurring only slowly then wider spans of control are found to exist.
(v) If the business has effective, efficient means of communication then misunderstandings will be less and spans will tend to be larger.
(vi) Finally, and possibly of the greatest importance, is the ability of the superior. A good delegator may be able to make decisions quickly and efficiently and so have a wide span of control.

If the span is too small then the organisation will be hampered by incomplete and insufficient delegation. Managers will over-control their juniors, interfering with their day-to-day work. If the span is excessive then subordinates may be poorly briefed, supported, trained and controlled. The manager will be overloaded and unable to make effective major decisions. Perhaps worse than this, he will not be able to process with speed the more minor problems and queries coming his way. The result will be a bottleneck causing frustration to subordinates as their own efficiency will be impaired. When this occurs, juniors may question the ability and competence of the manager to do his own job. Such a lack of confidence is dangerous to all concerned.

Levels of hierarchy

We saw earlier in the chapter the formal organisational structure of a medium size manufacturing company. We can see from fig. 3.1 that there was a vertical hierarchy of six levels of management (excluding the owners/shareholders). Such a 'tall' system of management is becoming increasingly unfashionable. Many businesses, even large ones are attempting to close the gap between the top and bottom. In this way the ideals and motivation of the leader will directly affect a larger number of people. Such moves may unify the business and enable those at the bottom of the hierarchy to feel more involved in the business. The more the number of levels involved then the greater will be the amount of filtering of information. Somewhat like the game of Chinese whispers, where a short message is passed secretly from one person to another. By the time the message gets to the fifth or sixth person the meaning and very nature of the message will have changed greatly. Missing out several levels between is also no answer as this will leave superiors ill-informed and lacking in authority over their subordinates.

What any effective hierarchy requires is sound, quick and effective communications and certainly computerisation, electronic mail and the use of high technology have done much to improve the flow of information both upwards and downwards in an organisation.

Task

Take an organisation of ten people, with a span of control of three, how many levels of hierarchy exist? Now compare this with an organisation of 1000 people with a span of control of four. How many extra levels of authority are needed?

3.8 Centralisation versus Decentralisation

Finally, the internal organisation of a business will be affected by the degree of centralisation or decentralisation allowed within the organisation. Centralisation refers to the amount of control exercised from the headquarters (or centre) compared to the amount of control left in the hands of the branches or departments of the business. Thus, if a company such as a large retail chain, issues very strict and specific instructions to its shop managers about staffing, stock control or fixtures and fittings, it will be considered to have a high degree of centralisation. Alternatively, if the business allows its managers the freedom to make independent decisions without reference to the central office, then it will be thought to have a large degree of decentralisation or autonomy.

The issue of the degree of centralisation has had many differing trends since the second world war. As an example The Rover Group has gone through a number of distinct phases. At times it was a loose collection of firms in the automotive industry, where each division was allowed to follow its own policy in pursuit of sales and profit. At other times the management of The Rover Group established a firm collective hold over the various parts of the business, establishing targets, advertising corporately and having a common policy on wages and salaries.

Any business will look towards a balance between the two conflicting directions of centralisation and decentralisation and these include:

(i) The need for a uniform policy on such issues as pricing or wage negotiations may be important. Most people would expect that a shirt purchased in a branch of a retail chain would bear the same cost as in another branch.
(ii) The cost of mistakes, particularly of spending limits may involve centralised decision-making to avoid waste or extravagance by one area of the business.
(iii) History. Businesses which have grown through mergers and takeovers are often more decentralised than those which have grown from within.
(iv) Geography. This is not as important a factor since the advent of modern communications systems. Businesses which were spread over a wide area of the globe were often forced to allow individual divisions to make their own decisions and policies, with little reference to the head office.
(v) Ability of management. While centralised businesses take much of the major decision-making out of the hands of middle and lower management, there is not such a need for talented managers. Decentralised businesses however, will only survive if those in the more junior ranks can effectively make independent and well considered decisions.
(vi) Personality of the senior managers. It is often the case that businesses who appoint highly publicised figure-heads will also be those where centralisation is a feature.

Fig. 3.7
Delegation, span of control and levels of hierarchy

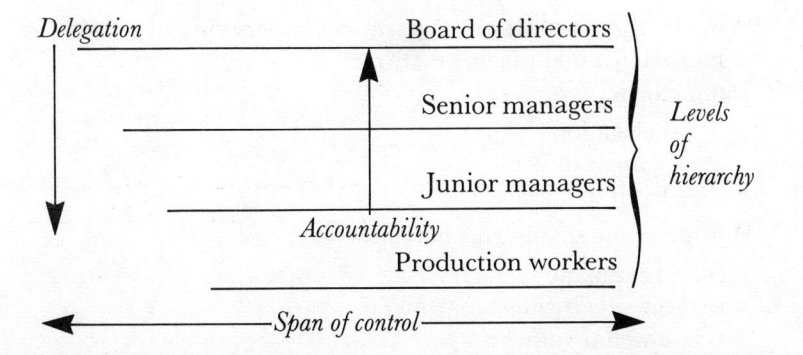

Test Yourself

Using the appropriate words from the bottom of this exercise, fill in the blank spaces in the following sentences.

1. A...... is the senior manager of any business.
2. Usually the...... employs the largest number of the company's employees.
3. The profit and loss account and balance sheet are drawn up by the ......
4. Management Accountants provide...... which helps decision-making at all levels.
5. The...... position of the firm is in the hands of the Company Secretary.
6. The recruitment officer helps to match future...... to positions in the firm.
7. Management Services provide...... and administrative support to the whole business.
8. ...... requires a manager to have trust in his ......
9. ...... is the number of people who report directly to one manager.
10. Many retail chain stores have a large degree of ......

legal   delegation   span of control   director   back-up

financial accountant   subordinates   production department

information   employees   centralisation

Questions

1. Why is the production department where most people are employed in a manufacturing firm?
2. Define the terms:
    —delegation
    —span of control
    —levels of hierarchy.
3. Why do many small firms not have:
    (i) a company secretary?
    (ii) an advertising department?
    (iii) a welfare officer?

4 What is the difference between the work of a financial accountant and a management accountant?
5 What are the drawbacks of a large firm pursuing a policy of decentralisation?
6 Analyse the problems associated with a firm attempting to reduce its levels of hierarchy.

PART II

BUSINESS BEHAVIOUR

Chapter 4

The Market

It is vital to any business of whatever size or type that it has a knowledge of the market into which it will sell its goods.

4.1 Finding a Market for your Product/Service

The business will want to know such information as:

—what type of people will buy the product;
—how many people will wish to purchase the product;
—how often customers will wish to purchase the product and in what quantities;
—where are these people likely to buy the product;
—what competition already exists for the product;
—what methods of marketing will provide the greatest encouragement to induce people to purchase the product.

Much of this information can be gained by carrying out *market research*. The term 'market research' is used to describe a number of techniques and research methods involved in discovering the characteristics of a particular market.

The cheapest type of market research is known as *desk research*, where information from government statistics and trade associations are analysed to gain an insight into the market. This type of information is usually of a very general nature and, while easy and cheap to collect, often does not provide the detailed insight into the market that a company requires. More specific information can be obtained by carrying out field research. Such work is often given to specialist market research agencies employed by the company. Much of this research is done through the completion of questionnaires by members of the public.

Techniques involved in market research

Many people have experienced market researchers at first hand, when approached in a shopping precinct by an interviewer holding a clipboard and being invited to '. . . answer a few questions'. Less popular but increasingly frequent is the use of telephone and postal research. These methods can cause annoyance to the recipient who sees them as an infringement upon their privacy. Even more annoying is the use of the term market research to disguise a sales campaign. True market research, however, should always be conducted professionally, scientifically and objectively if it is to be successful.

The questionnaire

The usual market research questionnaire should have the following features:

(a) A title and preamble — as most questionnaires are undertaken voluntarily, skill is required to get people to take part. Thus the purpose of the survey should be given in the opening paragraph.
(b) Length — an overlong questionnaire (more than 15 questions) will put people off and take additional time in the analysis of the results.
(c) Individual questions should be easy to understand, avoid offence, not require excessive calculation or memory work and allow easy analysis (this often means the use of boxes for ticking several alternatives).
(d) Layout should be clear and professional in its appearance.

Task

Using the hints given above, draw up a market research questionnaire of your own. The product or service may be an original idea of your own or a new brand of an existing product.

The sample — who to ask

The ideal market research would question the total population, but obviously for reasons of time and finance this is impossible. A sample of the population is taken which hopefully will reflect the tastes and opinions of the whole population. Various sampling methods can be used to identify who to ask. These methods include:

(a) Systematic sampling where, for instance, every twentieth person passing a particular shop is asked to complete the questionnaire or every hundredth person in a telephone directory is called and invited to answer some questions.

(b) Cluster sampling where an interviewer questions all the people in a particular street or who work in a specific firm. This type of sampling may be very cheap, however it may produce results which are biased.
(c) Stratified sampling is used when a firm wishes to get a fair balance of opinion from people within a particular population. Thus if you wished to know of the age of the people who may be potential purchasers of your product your interviewer would be asked to collect information from various age groups in proportion to the numbers of people within those age groups in the population as a whole.
(d) Quota sampling where those questioned reflect certain characteristics known to exist within the market, e.g. if it is known that 80% of all car oil is purchased by men between the age of 18-40 then 80% of the questionnaires would be given to men within this age group.

Analysis of results

Once the many questionnaires have been completed, the firm will wish to make some meaning of the results. Computer and statistical techniques are often used to analyse the results. The type of information gained may include:

—the size of the potential market;
—the average age and range of ages of potential buyers;
—the likely price the purchaser may be prepared to pay;
—the social and income groups of potential purchasers;
—the strengths and weaknesses of competitors products;
—the likely shopping habits of potential buyers.

Market research has therefore allowed the firm to build up a picture of its market. It is also the basis of forecasting the volume of sales and possible profitability of the product to the firm.

4.2 Selling the Product/Service

From the information gained from the firm's market research, the business will be in a position to identify the type of person who may purchase the product/service. It now needs to bring the product to the attention of these potential customers. This is done through the many techniques involved in advertising.

Reasons for advertising

Firms when spending money on advertising have two main goals:

(a) To *inform* potential customers of the many aspects of their product, i.e. its price, quality, availability, size, etc. Typically informative adverts are those found in the classified section of local and national newspapers.

(b) To *persuade* potential customers to buy their product as opposed to those of their competitors. TV advertising is often of a persuasive kind, where an image of the product or its purchaser is conveyed. The viewer associates this image with the product and by repetition and reinforcement the public may make a purchase of the product, and subsequent purchases.

Large corporations are increasingly using corporate advertising to convey an image of the corporation's identity rather than of any specific product.

The marketing mix

Advertising is a vital part of the business of trying to persuade people to buy a product but it is only one part of the marketing of a product. In all there are four aspects of the total marketing 'package' of a product known collectively as the marketing mix.

Fig. 4.1

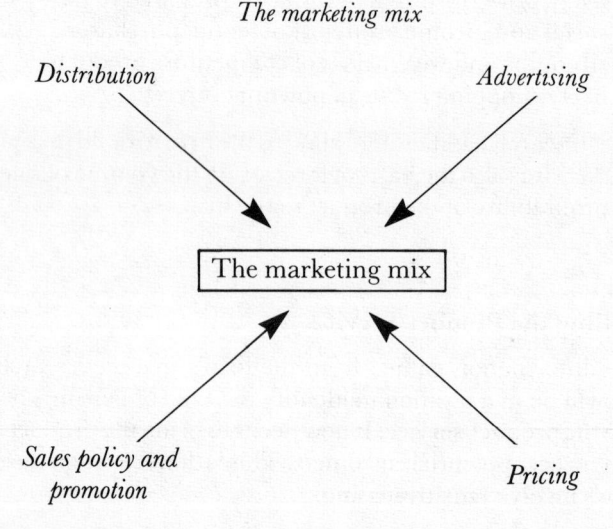

The marketing mix

Distribution → The marketing mix ← *Advertising*

Sales policy and promotion → The marketing mix ← *Pricing*

(a) *Distribution* — how the product is brought physically to the consumer. The traditional method is through the typical chain of distribution:

MANUFACTURER/PRODUCER→ WHOLESALER→ RETAILER→ CONSUMER

Often the producer may wish to have greater influence upon the outlet for its products. In this case he may wish to avoid one of the middlemen (the wholesaler and retailer) and to deal with a specific retailer or to sell through cash-and-carry warehouses, discount warehouses, mail order companies or through direct selling in newspapers. It may encourage retailers to stock its products by allowing favourable credit arrangements on its products. But, as any producer is aware, only by getting the product to the final point-of-sale will he sell his output, and thus the distribution of the product is a vital part of a company's marketing strategy.

(b) *Advertising* is designed to inform and persuade potential customers often creating an image for the product.

(c) *Sales and promotion* — the producer needs to decide how he intends to sell his products into the 'trade' and to the final consumer. Factors such as the size of the sales force, sales incentive schemes for representatives, organisation and management of sales force will all have an impact upon sale volume.

(d) *Pricing* — the decision over the pricing of a product is a vital one as it will have a substantial impact upon volume of sales and therefore sale revenue. When a product is selling in a competitive market where close substitutes exist then price will play a significant part in any sales campaign. Often as part of a marketing campaign a firm will attempt to differentiate its product from those of rivals in a hope of reducing the influence of the price of the product in the eyes of the consumer.

Products which have no close rivals or substitutes show that their price has less influence upon sales.

The product life cycle

Just as living things have a typical life cycle developing through the stages of birth, growth, maturity and finally death, these stages can also be identified in products. This phenomenon is known as the product life cycle. The various stages of this life cycle can be broken up into the following stages:

I   The firm researches the market for a product and makes the necessary adaptations and modifications to the product. The firm will consider 'launching' the product on the public through its wholesale and retail outlets. Ideally it will aim to have the product available and on display in the shops at the same time as its first wave of advertising occurs.

II The newly launched product, aided by extensive advertising, and initial interest and curiosity will face increasing sales by volume and amount of revenue. Slowly these initial increases will begin to fall away until sales reach a constant level.

III The product sales have now reached a plateau, and it has become an established consumer product with regular and consistent customers. The extent of advertising at this stage will diminish, as it is simply being used to reinforce consumer awareness of the product.

IV Competitors may develop similar products or introduce new versions of the product and take existing custom away from the original product. The product may also face a change of consumer tastes and preferences which originally had worked in the company's favour. Such changes may mean a fall in sales as consumer spending habits move to other products.

V The firm has to decide that the life of the product has now ended as they concentrate their energies on developing new ideas and models or they may consider extending the life cycle of the original product with a series of extension strategies, these may include such devices as:

(i)   A new advertising campaign.
(ii) A relaunch of the product with a different style of packaging, and promotions.
(iii) Introduce free gift, special offers or competitions.
(iv) Reduce the price of the product in an attempt to stimulate demand and perhaps attract customers from competitors' products.
(v)   Promote the product in new markets to a wider range of customers than had been the original intention of the product. This may include selling the product overseas.

These various stages can be seen in Fig. 4.2.

While this diagram illustrates what may happen to the revenue/volume of sales of the product it should not be confused with the profitability of the product. It is usual that in the early stages of the product's life cycle the costs incurred in production and marketing are much higher. Original research and development costs as well as the costs of purchasing equipment, machinery and expertise are all more

Fig. 4.2

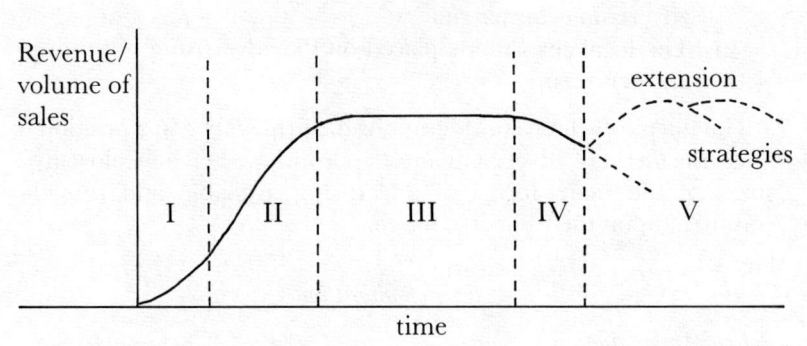

The product life cycle

expensive in the developmental phases of the product's life cycle. The diagram below illustrates the typical pattern of profits obtained from a product.

Fig. 4.3

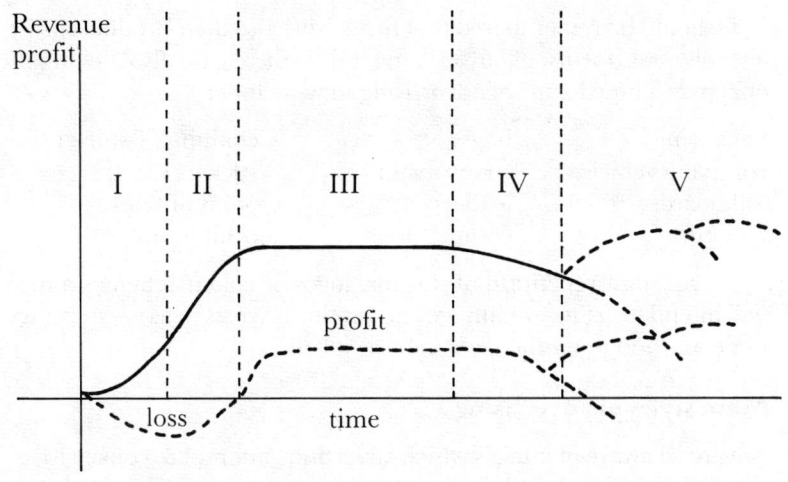

The product life cycle — with profits

The main types of advertising

Advertising takes many forms. A business will need to decide which methods are most appropriate to its products and image. The following points will be considered:

(i) The type of product.
(ii) The likely customers/consumers.

(iii) The potential anticipated demand for the product.
(iv) The amount of money that is being budgeted for the advertising campaign.
(v) The legal constraints placed on the advertising of products and services.

Having made these considerations the firm will be in a position to select the forms of advertising most appropriate. Fig. 4.4 below gives some of the main forms of advertising available and provides comment upon their possible usage.

Fig. 4.4

Types of advertising

Type of Advertising	Cost	Coverage	Range
Local newspapers	cheap	local	limited
National newspapers	expensive	national	wide
General magazines	expensive	national	wide
Specialist magazines	moderate	national	selective
Independent TV	very expensive	local/national	wide
Commercial radio	moderate	local	wide

It should be remembered that firms advertise their products using less obvious forms of advertising but which can also be highly effective. These forms of advertising may include:

packaging	bags	clothing (T-shirts)
company vehicles	sponsorship	stickers (cars)
bill boards	leaflets	point of sales
free gifts	competitions	exhibitions

By constant repetition of slogans, logos or colour schemes a firm will intend to get its own image and products across to as wide a range of people and potential customers as it can.

Main styles of advertising

We are all aware of images which advertisers attempt to convey to us. Advertisers often use their adverts to persuade potential customers that the product will make the consumer better off in some way. A number of common styles and images can be identified from an examination of magazines, newspapers and TV adverts. These images often fall into the following categories:

(i) Sex appeal — where the product claims to make the consumer more attractive to the opposite sex.

(ii) Personality appeal — the advert shows a famous sporting or media personality using or praising the product. The personality and the product become inseparable in the eyes of the consumer.
(iii) Success appeal — where a product is linked with an image of an apparently successful person. The implication is that some of the success came from the person's use of the product.
(iv) Task simplification — by showing a person with greater leisure time due to the use of the product.

Task

Taking the following products and services, identify the appropriate types of advertising and the style of advertising. Be prepared to explain your answers:

— a new breakfast cereal;
— a new style of dishwasher;
— a local insurance broker;
— a second-hand car;
— a new perfume;
— a small engineering business.

The use and functions of advertising agencies

Only the largest firms can afford to have their own advertising departments who plan and co-ordinate the advertising campaign. Most companies will employ specialist advertising agencies who for a fee or commission will devise, manage and advise the firm on its marketing policy and the development of its products. The work of an advertising agency specifically involves the following activities:

(i) To carry out the market research and analyse the results from such research to assess the potentials of the market.
(ii) The art department will be involved in drawing up the pictorial display of the advertisement and the wording/slogans which will accompany it. The use of catch phrases or jingles is an important part of many advertising campaigns.
(iii) Once the product is available in substantial quantities and the advertising for both final consumer and the 'trade' is ready, then the marketing campaign is ready to be launched on the public. This launch and the subsequent weeks and months of the campaign will be managed by the agency. They will need to 'buy space' in newspapers and on TV. The advertising

budget will allow for substantial spending in the early stages of the campaign during the development stage of the product's life cycle and tailing off during the later stages of the product's life. The agency, in consultation with the company, may recommend renewed expenditure if sales fall as one of the extension strategies the company may wish to employ.

4.3 Consumer Protection

Why the consumer needs protection

Producers of goods and services use a variety of techniques to persuade and inform customers about their products. Marketing methods can also confuse and sometimes mislead consumers about the qualities and properties of their products. Over many years through the work of pressure groups and governments, consumers have been provided with a number of forms of protection against companies who overstep the mark in terms of the methods they use to sell their products.

Consumer protection fits into a number of separate categories:

(a) *Acts of Parliament*

There are many laws which affect and protect the consumer but the following are the main ones:

  (i) Food Act 1984. Under this act it is an offence to sell food which is unfit for human consumption. It also regulates food hygiene including places where food is sold and prepared.
  (ii) Weights and Measures Act 1963. This act makes it an offence to sell short weight or incorrectly mark the weight of pre-packed items.
  (iii) The Trades Descriptions Act 1968. This act makes it an offence for a trader to falsely describe the goods or services he is offering.
  (iv) Unsolicited Goods and Services Act 1971. This act makes it illegal for a trader to demand payment for goods supplied which people have not ordered. It also gives the recipient the right to keep the goods if they remain uncollected after six months.
  (v) Sale of Goods Act as amended by the Supply of Goods Act (Implied Terms) 1973. These acts make it illegal to sell goods which are not of merchantable quality, i.e. not fit for the

purpose for which they were sold. The act also insists that goods must be as described by the packaging, advertisement or salesman. If a customer has a complaint under this act then he should return the goods to the retailer from whom he originally purchased them, and with whom he made the original contract of sale. In the case of faulty goods the consumer is not obliged to accept a credit note but may insist upon a cash refund.

(vi) The Consumer Credit Act 1974. This wide ranging act is designed to control all those who offer credit to consumers. It regulates such matters as the cancellation of credit agreements, the providing of information concerning interest rates and periods of repayment as well as providing recourse to those misrepresented by credit reference agencies.

(b) *Government and local authority departments*

(i) Trading standards/consumer protection departments. These organisations investigate complaints about wrong descriptions or the wrong quantity of goods supplied. They have the authority to prosecute retailers on behalf of individual consumers for faulty goods or poor service.

(ii) Environmental health department. These departments deal with complaints associated with health matters, for example unhygienic butchers, bakers and restaurants.

(iii) Consumer advice centres. Many local authorities operate these centres, where free advice on a wide range of consumer matters can be obtained by members of the public. They are situated in or near to large shopping areas.

(iv) The Office of Fair Trading. This was set up under the Fair Trading Act of 1973, and a director-general of fair trading was appointed to oversee the work of this government agency. The function of the OFT is to provide the consumer with information about their rights and to ensure that their interests are being looked after. The director-general often makes recommendations to government about new laws which should be introduced to further protect the consumer.

(c) *Consumer agencies and organisations*

(i) The Consumer Association publishes the 'Which' magazine, and many satellite publications. Its members through their subscriptions receive a copy of this publication which provides guidance to consumers upon their choice of goods and services. The association tests and investigates many products and may recommend 'best buys'. It is also a powerful pressure group representing consumers and their interests. In this role it is often listened to by government when drafting consumer legislation.

(ii) The British Standards Institute (BSI). This is an independent organisation which lays down minimum standards necessary for products to be fit for the purpose for which they were intended.

The Kitemark on a product is an indication to consumers that it has met certain standards. The re-testing of products ensures that goods maintain the required standard or face the consequences of losing the Kitemark.

The safety mark is also awarded by the BSI where products have been tested by the Institute and are found to meet minimum standards of safety. Such marks can commonly be seen on fire-proofed furniture, motor cycle crash helmets and children's clothing.

(iii) The Design Council is an organisation partly funded by government. The council chooses products that have been well made, are of pleasant appearance and practical to use. They allow the producer to display the Design Council's label on its products.

(iv) Professional and trade associations try to get their members to agree to abide by a voluntary code of practice when dealing with consumers. Often they establish a fund to compensate aggrieved consumers when one of their members is unable or unwilling to meet their responsibilities.

(v) Nationalised industries consumer/consultative councils

provide a similar function as trade associations but in respect of nationalised industries. They offer help and advice to those consumers who are having difficulties with such organisations as the Post Office, British Rail, etc.

(vi) The Advertising Standards Authority is a specialist watchdog organisation which exerts pressure on its members to withdraw adverts which do not meet the basic principle of their code of 'legal, decent, honest and truthful'. If a complaint is made to the authority by a member of the public it will be investigated and some satisfactory result achieved.

Test Yourself

Using the appropriate words from the bottom of this exercise, fill in the blank spaces in the following sentences.

1. Market research often involves the use of . . . . . . to ask members of the public their opinions about a product.
2. Advertising can be used to . . . . . . and . . . . . . potential customers.
3. The marketing mix includes advertising . . . . and . . . . . .
4. The middlemen in the chain of distribution include the . . . . . . and . . . . . .
5. A 'special offer' on an existing product may be a type of . . . . . .
6. A specialist . . . . . . may be employed by a firm to organise its advertising campaign.
7. The Sale of Goods Act makes it illegal for goods to be sold which are not of . . . . . .
8. The . . . . . . is the symbol of the British Standards Institute.
9. 'Legal, decent, honest and truthful' is the motto of the . . . . . .
10. The Fair Trading Act (1973) set up the . . . . . .

Advertising Standards Authority   Office of Fair Trading

advertising agency   merchantable quality   distribution

retailer   extension strategy   questionnaire   inform

sales policy and promotion   persuade   pricing   wholesaler

Kitemark

Questions

1. List as many forms of advertising in common use as you can.
2. Why does the consumer need the protection of the law to safeguard his interests?
3. You have bought a jumper over the weekend which when opened was found to have a tear in the sleeve. The shop is refusing to take the item back. Write a letter to an appropriate consumer agency clearly stating all the relevant information. What action or advice do you think they are likely to give?
4. Using the illustration of either a motor car or a new kind of hi-fi equipment, explain the stages of the product's life cycle.
5. Describe the way that an advertising campaign for a new type of chocolate bar is likely to unfold.

Chapter 5

Producing the Product

Case example: Jaguar Cars is a large manufacturer of cars. Often its products are sold to the export market, particularly in the United States of America. Jaguar designs, produces and sells a variety of models in the upmarket category. The company buys in many components and adds these to the items produced in its own workshops. The process of assembly is along a production line where a highly skilled workforce, using sophisticated equipment, produces the high quality end product.

Such a system of manufacture is similar to that found in thousands of companies. Production is the transformation of raw materials or components into end products using labour, capital (money), machinery, materials and energy.

Fig. 5.1

$$\left.\begin{array}{l}\text{Labour}\\\text{Capital}\\\text{Machinery}\\\text{Materials}\\\text{Energy}\end{array}\right\} \text{Production} \left\{\begin{array}{l}\text{Product}\\\\\text{Waste}\end{array}\right.$$

5.1 Production and Specialisation

A characteristic of modern production is the amount of specialisation which occurs. This is the process where one worker undertakes a very particular task, often repetitively, on the factory floor. Such a system of working can be traced back to the industrial revolution of the eighteenth and nineteenth centuries. Before this time the United Kingdom was basically an agricultural society. The population lived and worked on the land; families were self-sufficient in that most of what was needed they provided for themselves, or went without.

During the late eighteenth century many people moved off the land into the growing towns and cities, looking for work in the new factories.

Factory work meant that the workers could no longer produce what they needed. Instead the factory owner employed them in jobs which they repeated many times each day; they eventually became specialists. For such work they were paid a wage from which they could purchase the food, clothing and housing that their families needed.

The factory system is an example of the division of labour. Instead of each person trying to produce everything they needed themselves, they specialised. This specialisation allowed more to be produced per worker, rather than each worker trying to do several jobs at once. Such specialisation came under the scrutiny of Adam Smith, often reputed to be the first economist. In his *Wealth of Nations* (1776) he observed two distinct methods of producing pins. One system was the old cottage industry method where a group of workers each carried out all the separate tasks of pin production. While in a factory a similar number of people each specialised in one task of the pin production process. Smith noted a tenfold increase in production using the factory system and provided much of the academic support for this method of producing goods.

Today the advantages of specialisation are still to be seen. Two main reasons for the efficiency of specialisation can be noted.

(i) Workers became very skilled at their jobs. Doing the same task repetitively they became very expert. Able to work out short-cuts to make their jobs easier and quicker.

(ii) Less time is lost moving between jobs. The workers will have all the tools they need close by and they will be able to settle down quickly to their jobs.

Such benefits have given rise to the mass production methods we associate with many companies. Production is fast and efficient, resulting in greater output and profit. The output of a firm against the cost of producing goods can be seen in Fig. 5.2 accompanying the case example which follows:

Case example: Smithfield Ltd. makes and sells sweets to the confectionery trade. It employs 40 workers on a production line, each being a specialist in a particular type of work, mixing, stacking, coating, packing. The management of Smithfields is aware that when sales are low they still have to pay these direct workers their wages — about £5000 per week. They also know that other costs such as lighting, heating, rates and administration add another £2500 per week. All of these costs have to be met, irrespective of the number of boxes sold. These costs (called fixed costs — see Chapter 7) can be added to the cost of the ingredients of the sweets, which work out at 50 pence for each box. So when the firm was thriving, just before Easter, in one week it sold 15 000 boxes. The cost of this was:

Direct workers' wages	£5000
Administration, etc.	£2500
+ 15 000 @ 50p	£7500
	£15 000

Thus the average cost for each box was:

$$\frac{\text{Total Cost}}{\text{Quantity}} = \frac{£15\,000}{15\,000} = £1.00 \text{ per box.}$$

Later in the year the firm only sold 10 000 boxes in a week. Its total costs = £12 500 (make sure you can see how this is calculated).

The average cost in this week was therefore:

$$\frac{£12\,500}{10\,000} = £1.25$$

From other information about sales the firm could see that the higher the sales were, the lower was the average cost of each box. This gives rise to a downward sloping average cost curve, which looks like this:

Fig. 5.2
The average cost curve of Smithfields Sweets Ltd.

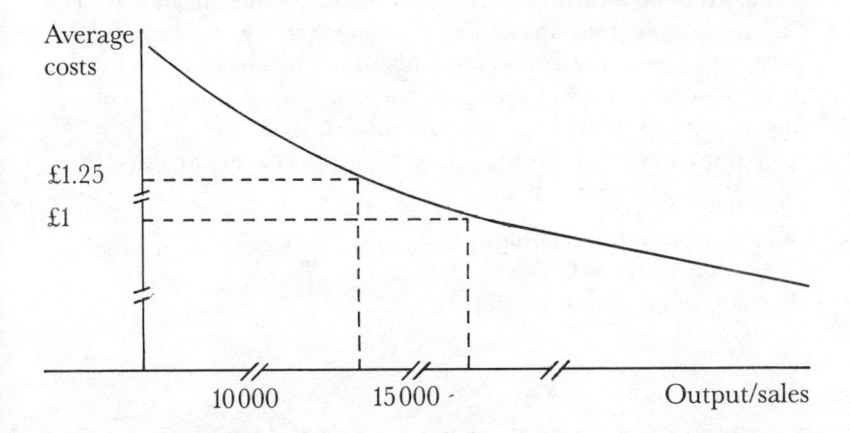

This gives us another advantage of specialisation, for it can be seen that the greater the level of output then the lower will be the average or unit cost.

Specialisation inevitably has some disadvantages, particularly to the worker. Constant repetition of the same task can become boring and monotonous. Often the workers' speed of performance is determined by the rate of progress of the production line or 'track'. This can build up natural frustration as workers feel that they cannot control their own working speed. Workers have been known to literally 'put a spanner in the works' to stop or slow down the track, to relieve the tedium of the work. Often factories with production lines are prone to industrial action. Each worker or group knows that without them performing their tasks the whole factory can be brought to a standstill. If workers are bored by what they are expected to do, they may seek short cuts in completing the job. This can result in a poor quality end product. Ultimately, if the task becomes so specialised then there may be no reason why it cannot be totally automated. The feature of many production lines is the absence of people carrying out the routine jobs and being replaced by computerised machines. Such methods have created large amounts of job losses in the traditional high employment manufacturing industries.

5.2 Production Methods

We have seen how large motor manufacturers use production line methods. Of course this is not the only method of producing cars. Some car manufacturers who deal in specialist low-volume vehicles will often build a car to a particular customer's specifications. Each car is different from any other; a unique vehicle in its own right. Between these two extreme methods of car production are the car manufacturers who will produce short-runs of the same model and then transfer production to another model.

Within these three descriptions it is possible to identify three distinct production methods:

—job or unit production;
—batch production;
—flow or line production.

Job production

Job production is concerned with making one-off items. Often the firms involved in such unit production are small, employing highly skilled specialist craftsmen. Examples of such methods could be found in cabinet/furniture makers or specialist precision engineers.

However, a large ship-building or construction company may argue that they are producing one-off items.

What these examples have in common are a number of features which set job production apart. These include:

—high skill level
—versatile workforce
—flexible machinery and equipment which can perform a range of tasks
—setting up the job, checking and obtaining a quality finish take up the bulk of production time.

Batch production

Batch production is a method of producing a number of similar components at the same time. Once a batch has been worked upon, it is passed on to the next stage of manufacture. The manufacture of steel castings typifies batch production. A group of moulds have molten steel poured into them at one time. They are allowed to cool, then the sand moulds are knocked off the casting. The batch is passed onto the fettling shop where pneumatic hammers knock off any excess sand and unwanted pieces of metal. Finally, the castings are machined to obtain the exact dimensions required.

Batch production may tie up machinery, workers and stock for a considerable period of time but it does allow a large degree of specialisation to take place. To ensure a high quality of output, batch production methods often involve inspection of parts at each stage of manufacture. Once a batch is complete then the machinery may be reset to carry out work on the next batch.

A batch may be anything from two components or parts to a run of several million small items. The size of the batch will depend on the customer's delivery requirements, the company's pattern of orders and the firm's production and storage capacity.

Flow or line production

Flow or line production as we have seen is typified by the car assembly plant but is also to be found in such continuous process industries as the chemical industry, many food production lines and oil refining. With this system of production each unit is passed on to the next process, uninterrupted, until it is complete.

Flow production shows the highest level of specialisation with each individual task broken into its smallest element. Such methods are increasingly using computerised machinery and are known as capital intensive production lines, requiring large amounts of plant and equipment to be used by each worker.

Output from these lines of production is highly standardised, each unit resembling all other units. To ensure that the products meet certain minimum standards, it is usual to have a large number of inspection engineers. It is their job to select a sample from the 'line' and to measure and test these items. If the sample meets the standards then the line is assured to be performing to the quality required. If the sample has faults, then it may mean resetting the machinery and rejection of a large quantity of output.

Flow production has, as we have seen, the great advantage of reducing unit costs (see Fig. 5.2). It also places many demands upon the organisation of the firm, these may include:

(i) Careful planning of production design to ensure that standardisation of parts is possible.
(ii) The demand for the final product must be large and constant. Production lines cannot be switched on and off at short notice.
(iii) Parts, components and raw materials need to be available in large supplies to ensure that shortages do not occur.
(iv) Maintenance of plant is designed to prevent breakdown not just to repair equipment when it fails.
(v) The workforce needs to be covered by additional staff in case of sickness, tea or toilet breaks.

5.3 The Location of Industry

One of the most important decisions any business takes is where to locate its many product plants. Careful siting will help to reduce costs and so help to maximise profits. Such decisions affect not only new companies but old established firms as well who may consider expansion and the location of their additional capacity.

The ideal location of any firm will depend upon the size of the company and the nature of its products. It will also depend upon a number of factors under the headings:

(i) The firm's market.
(ii) The closeness of raw materials.
(iii) The cost of land.
(iv) The requirements of appropriately skilled labour.
(v) The importance of energy.
(vi) The influence of transport costs.
(vii) The effects of government policies.

The firm's market

The firm's market may have significance to any business which needs to be close to its customers. Most service industries are described as market orientated, thus a garage will gain advantages being on a main road close to its potential customers.

Modern communications have increasingly meant that firms can distance themselves from their market without penalty. International telecommunications have meant that the market of many firms has been extended across country boundaries.

The closeness of raw materials

The closeness of raw materials is an essential factor of industries producing or processing primary products. Thus ironworks, flour mills and oil refineries tend to be close to the sources of their raw materials.

The cost of land

The cost of land will vary from place to place. If a firm requires a substantial acreage to build its factory then the cost of land will become an important consideration. Today it is common to find the newer industrial developments on the edge of towns and cities, where cheap land with planning permission can be obtained.

The requirements of appropriately skilled labour

Labour with appropriate skills becomes an important consideration to firms who require a particular type of workforce. When a firm requires metal workers it may seek premises near to the old ship-building centres of the North-East of England. A light engineering company making electronic components may consider the Midlands as an appropriate site, where many skilled workers are seeking employment.

It is often the case that companies involved in similar industries are situated in a concentrated area. The result can be devastating to a particular town when the industry faces a decline in demand for its products. High levels of unemployment may occur, often with people who are highly trained in very specific skills.

The importance of energy

The importance of an abundant power supply is not as vital as it used to be. Many of the old textile towns in the North of England were located close to both sources of water and of power and coal. Such requirements are no longer necessary as the national grid can deliver electricity to most parts of the country. Interestingly the manufacture of aluminium from bauxite requires vast quantities of electrical power and such plants are often close to the sources of hydroelectric power.

The influence of transport costs

The importance of transport costs and the method of transport is important to all manufacturing companies. Many firms are located close to the motorway network or have their own railway sidings. Firms involved in international trade find obvious benefits being close to either a major airport or to a port.

The effects of government policies

The effects of government policies may persuade firms to seek locations where the maximum amount of grant aid is available. Certain areas of the country have exceptionally high levels of unemployment.

The government has made attempts to relocate industries away from the relative prosperity of the South East to the areas of high unemployment in Northern Ireland, the North of England, Wales and the West Midlands. Such areas are eligible for a variety of grants and incentives to help firms consider these areas, known collectively as Development Areas. The benefits may include:
—cash grants for new machinery and buildings.
—purpose built factory units at low rentals.
—low interest loans to businesses.
—improved infrastructure, road, rail and air links.
—government financed retraining schemes such as TOPS courses (Training Opportunities Scheme) where free retraining can be undertaken, in an attempt to match the skilled labour requirements of the new industries.

It has to be said, however, that even with the good intentions of successive governments, the effects of regional policy have been disappointing. It is the case that the differences in regional unemployment have got worse rather than better over the last decade.

Other factors also have an influence upon location. For example: the siting of firms, due to the personal preferences of the chairman or managing director; the 'green field' developments of growing towns such as Milton Keynes, Telford New Town and Peterborough; and the retention of firms in an area when the original reason for its siting is no longer applicable (known as 'industrial inertia').

Task

Consider the following industries/businesses and try to match them up with one or two of the factors affecting location:

1. Car manufacturing.
2. Steel making.
3. A new retail hypermarket.
4. Poultry farm.
5. Insurance brokers.
6. Book publisher.
7. A new coal field.
8. A small electronics business, making specialist hi-fi equipment.

5.4 Factory Design

Having examined how firms decide upon their location, we can now look at how a company may organise its works.

Case study of Components Ltd

We shall consider the layout of a medium-sized engineering firm. The company employs 120 staff, making small electrical components for the radio, television and video industry. The firm is located on an industrial estate on the edge of a large Midlands town. It is close to both rail and good road links. A junction of the M6 is only four miles away. Its customers are spread throughout the country and the firm uses its own fleet of vehicles to deliver its goods. Recently it has opened up an export trade with a number of United States companies. Thus the closeness of an international airport at Birmingham has become important.

The raw materials are made up of brass and steel rods which are machined by a variety of semi-automatic machines. The firm uses batch production methods, a batch being anything from 100 components to 100 000 components. The direct workforce of 95 people work a three-shift system of eight hours. This means that the machinery is in constant use, except at weekends when 'preventative' maintenance takes place.

The indirect workers are employed in the offices and include a receptionist, four secretaries, four representatives working from their own homes, the production controller, five inspection engineers and the firm's three directors — one responsible for the accounts department, one for the sales team and the other in charge of production.

The stages involved in an order would be as follows:

(i) A representative, upon visiting an old customer, is asked to give a quotation to make 10000 small brass components to fit on the back of video sets.

(ii) The sales office prices the order, on the basis of materials used, and the labour involved. A 30% mark-up is then applied to give the profit from this order and cover indirect overheads (e.g. advertising, office expenses, etc.).

(iii) After negotiation between the representative and the customer's chief buyer a lower price for the order may then be agreed. The representative gives a firm delivery date of six weeks' time.

(iv) The production controller works out the appropriate timings involved in manufacturing the batch and three weeks before delivery he informs the production manager that work on the order should be started.

(v) The brass rods are loaded on to the machines, which are set to the appropriate cutting lengths.

(vi) Over the next five shifts the parts are manufactured, with reloading and resetting of the machines going on throughout this time.

(vii) The parts are put in metal crates in batches of 500 components. These crates are washed to remove stray pieces of brass and then passed into the inspection department.

(viii) From each crate a number are removed and tested to ensure that they meet the customer's specifications. If satisfied with the sample, the Inspector will pass the crate on for packaging. If some of his samples do not meet the requirements he will check and test some more. If these are found to be wrong then he will reject the whole batch and inform the production manager. The production manager will then investigate the problem, perhaps resetting the machines.

(ix) The whole consignment will now be ready for delivery to the customer and will await transport with another batch of parts going to a customer in a similar area.

(x) Once the customer has taken delivery he will do his own checks on the batch. If satisfied he will inform the accounts department, who will make payment when the invoice for the order becomes due.

Fig. 5.3

A plan of Components Ltd.

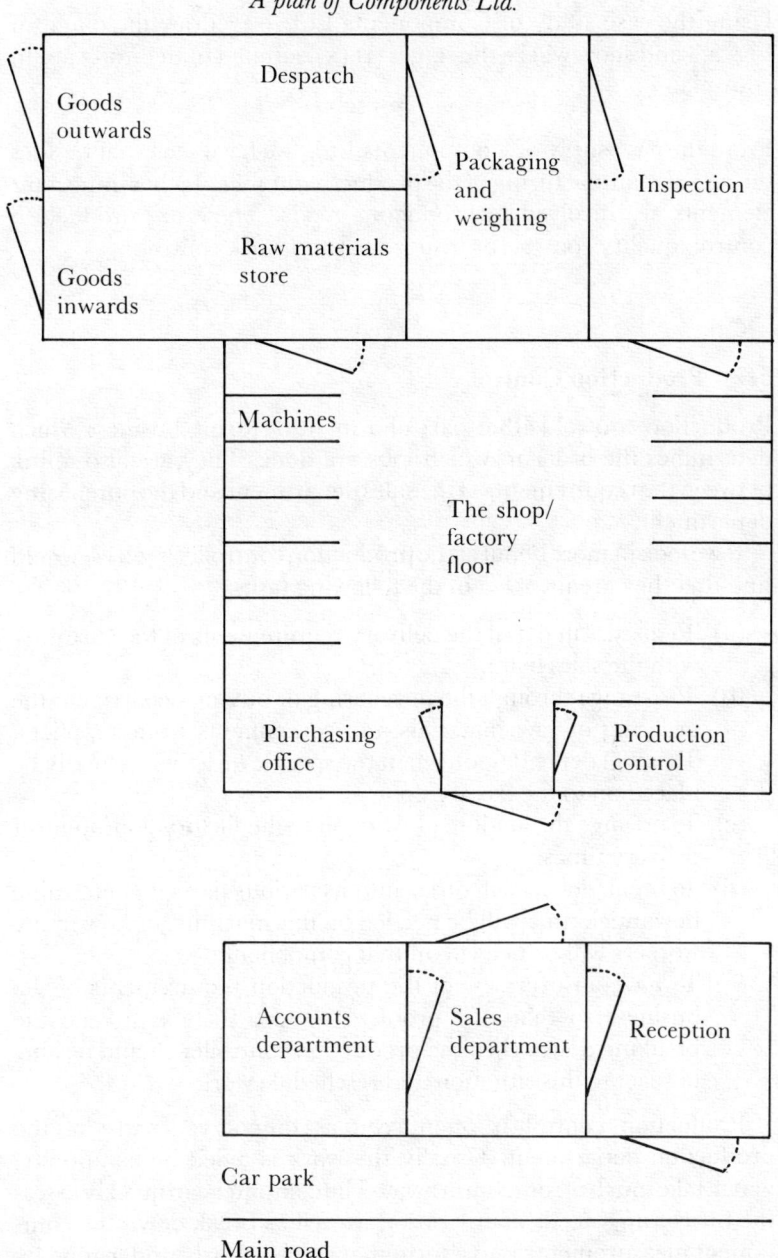

| Goods outwards | Despatch | Packaging and weighing | Inspection |
| Goods inwards | Raw materials store | | |

Machines

The shop/factory floor

Purchasing office — Production control

Accounts department | Sales department | Reception

Car park

Main road

Task

Using the case study of Components Ltd. — redraw the diagram Fig. 5.3 and show where the stages (i)-(x) outlined in the study are in your plan.

From the case study of Components Ltd., we have seen that besides the actual manufacturing of the product a number of other important elements are involved in producing goods. These are production control, quality control (or inspection) and stock control.

5.5 Production Control

Production control is that part of a manufacturing business which determines the order in which jobs are done. They are also a link between the requirements of the sales department and the purchasing department.

If we look in more detail at the production controller's job we would find that they are involved in the following tasks:

(a) To discuss in detail the delivery requirements of the customer with the sales team.
(b) To arrange through the purchasing or buying department the ordering of raw materials and components from suppliers. This will depend upon when the specific order will actually be placed on to the factory floor.
(c) To arrange the loading of work on to the factory floor to meet delivery times.
(d) To break down each order into its various parts, to determine how much time will be needed on this machine, or how many workers will be needed on that component.
(e) To have an overview of the production requirements of the business so that if a problem occurs, such as a machine breaking down, then the production controller should be able to react to this situation and reschedule work.

Production control is often seen as the nerve centre of the production department. Usually the work is aided by computers, which take much of the tedium away. The computer can quickly assess the purchasing needs of any order, as well as break down the component measurements into a form that can be clearly understood by the machinists on the factory floor.

5.6 Quality Control

Quality control (or inspection) was seen, traditionally, as simply the inspection of the finished product, to see whether the parts were within the customer's requirements. We have seen in the Components Ltd. case study how samples are taken to check the flow of work from the factory floor. Today, however, quality control is seen as a far wider area of production management. Indeed production control should look at all stages of the product's life, from its design, through manufacture to final delivery. Only in this way will goods be produced of a quality which will satisfy their customers.

In many industries quality control is an expensive part of the production process, yet without such control the firm would face poor quality output and the loss of custom. Money spent on quality is money well spent. The cost of quality can be attributed to the following:

—the cost of *replacing* an item already in the hands of a customer;
—the cost of *repairing* items still under guarantee;
—the cost of *inspecting*, sorting and testing items to ensure that they meet design specifications;
—the cost of *maintaining* equipment in good working order to prevent machinery turning out poor quality parts.

The important decision to be made by any business is how much should be spent on quality control. The greater the level of inspection and maintenance the higher the costs. Alternatively, if insufficient amounts are spent then the greater will be the costs of replacement and repair. Fig. 5.4 gives a model of the optional amount of quality control needed by a business.

Defective products may occur for a variety of reasons:

(i) The machinery making the item cannot produce the goods of the quality expected by the customer.
(ii) The design may call for too precise measurements which the firm's machinery cannot meet.
(iii) The operators may not have the time or methods of checking their output.
(iv) The worker may have no incentive or motivation to care about quality. This is particularly the case in flow or line production, when volume of output is linked to bonus payments with no penalties for sub-standard work.

It is for the firm's management to ensure that what they are asking

Fig. 5.4

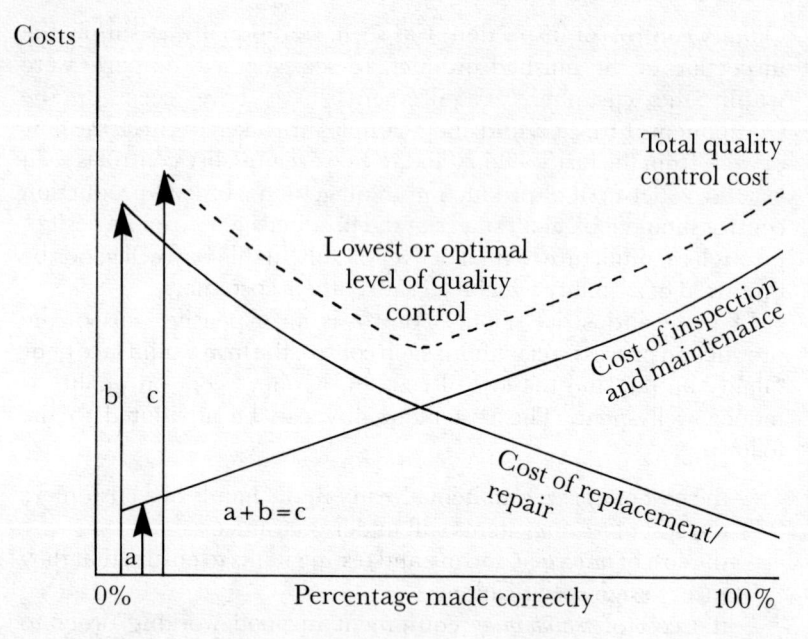

```
Costs
         Total quality control cost
         Lowest or optimal
         level of quality
         control
                              Cost of inspection
                              and maintenance
    b  c
                  Cost of replacement/
                  repair
         a+b=c
      a
0%         Percentage made correctly        100%
```

of both their machinery and workforce is within their capabilities. It is also a management problem to provide the motivation for production workers to be concerned about quality.

Task

Consider a product with which you have had cause for complaint.

  (a) What was the defect?
  (b) How do you think the defect occurred?
  (c) What might the Company have done to reduce the chances of such defects occurring?
  (d) What effect upon the reputation of the company, in your eyes, did the defect have?

5.7 Stock Control

The control of stock is an important aspect of production management, as it can account for considerable amounts of money. Some retail stores value their total stock as over 50% of their assets and this figure is similar in the textile, building, construction and civil engineering businesses. Reducing stock levels by as little as 10% in a particular firm may release many millions of pounds which could be used elsewhere in the business, e.g. new machines, developing a new product or engaging in a new advertising campaign.

The production department of any business would wish to play safe with its stocks. This often means expensive over-stocking and is at odds with the firm's overall objective of maximising profits.

Fig. 5.5

Types of stock

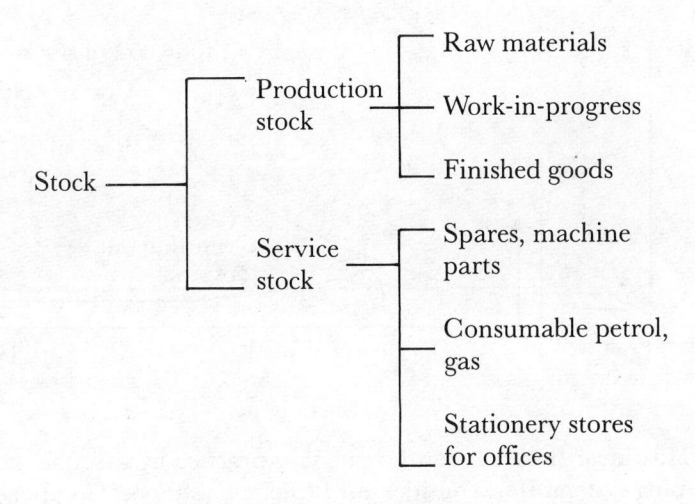

```
                    ┌─ Production ──┬─ Raw materials
                    │    stock      ├─ Work-in-progress
                    │               └─ Finished goods
Stock ──────────────┤
                    │               ┌─ Spares, machine
                    │               │   parts
                    └─ Service ─────┼─ Consumable petrol,
                         stock      │   gas
                                    └─ Stationery stores
                                        for offices
```

Task

Consider the stocks of items which you have at home. (Tins of foods, freezer foods, stationery, garden items, do-it-yourself items, etc.)

1 Into what categories do these stocks fall? (see Fig. 5.5).
2 In what items do you consider you are over-stocked?
3 How do you know whether you are over-stocked?
4 How much money is tied up in these stocks? (A rough estimate will do.)
5 How else could this money have been spent without affecting the smooth running of the household?

How then does a company attempt to control its stock? As with the problem of quality control, holding stock has a variety of costs. Firstly there is the cost of the stock itself. Then the cost of running out of appropriate stock needs to be considered. This may involve waiting for stocks to arrive and having workers under-used, also machines not working. Customers may face delays in delivery and seek supplies from elsewhere. The optimal level of stock can be illustrated using Figs. 5.6 and 5.7 where the cost of stocks can be placed under two headings:

(i) *The cost of holding stock* will naturally increase with high levels of stock.
(ii) *The cost of running out of stock* will reduce with high levels of stock.

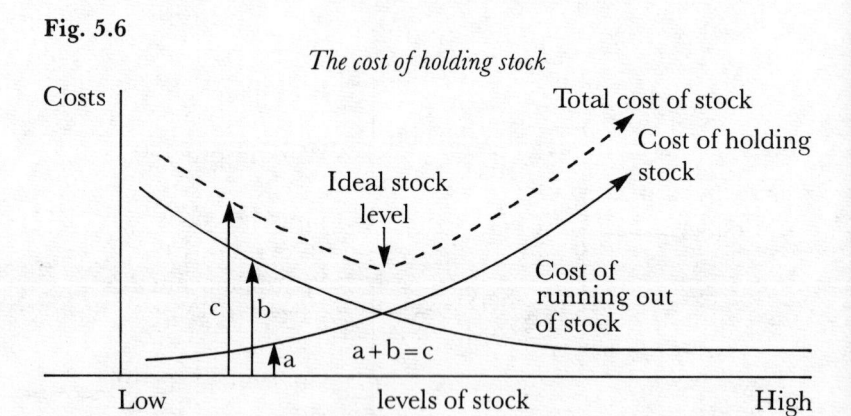

Fig. 5.6

The cost of holding stock

This ideal situation can be put into practice by a sound stock-keeping system. If we consider our earlier case study of Components Ltd., we note that its main raw material stocks are rods of brass and steel. Let us now see how they carry out their stock control.

Case study of Components Ltd. stock control system

When a firm order is received from a customer, the production controller will inform the purchasing department of the order requirements. The purchasing department is aware of the level of stock of all types of materials. They will consider the timing of the order and the amounts required. They know that their supplier needs two weeks' notice for a delivery to be made and that the minimum size of the delivery is 100 rods and a maximum of 500. The stock controller will also inform the purchasing department when any type of rod falls below a level of 200; this is called the re-order level. Below is a pattern of stock holding for a particular type of brass rod within Component's Ltd.

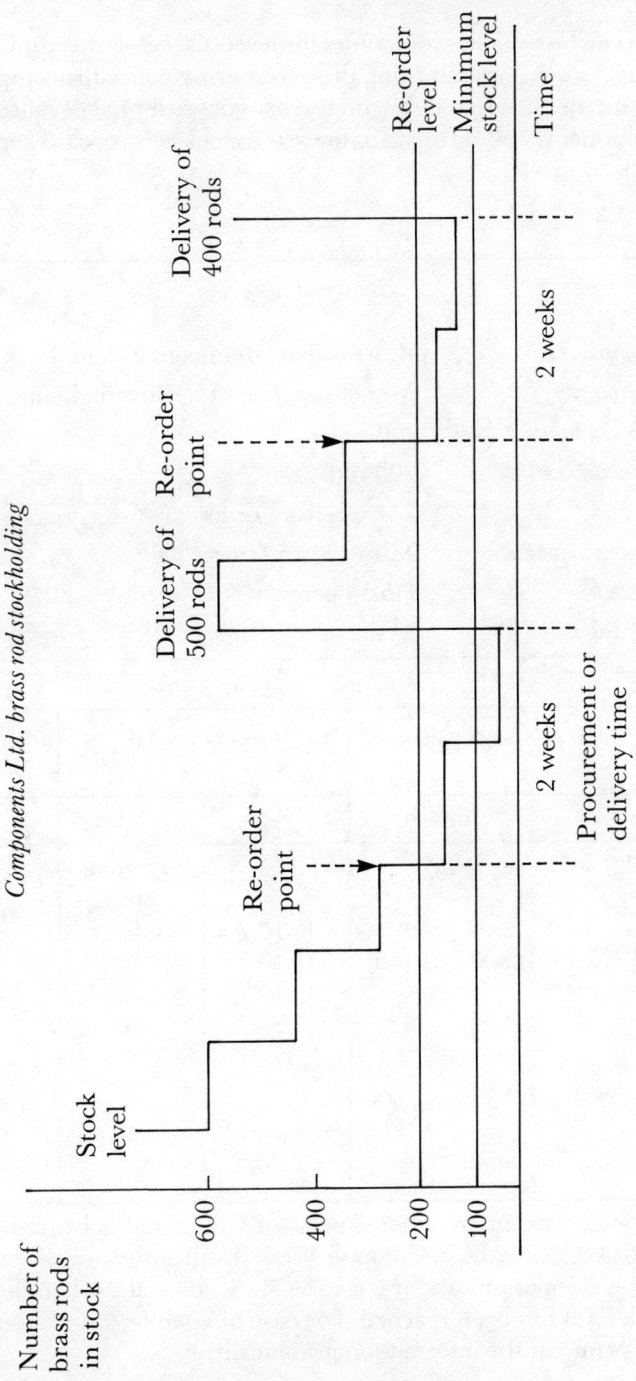

Fig. 5.7
Components Ltd. brass rod stockholding

It can be seen that sometimes the levels fall below the minimum (or buffer) stock level but using this re-ordering policy the company has never run out of vital raw materials. For each type of material and component used by the firm there is a stock control card kept by the stock controller.

Fig. 5.8

	Brass rod stock card
Components:	Brass rods 1″ diameter, 6″ length
Supplier:	Metal Supplier Ltd., Birmingham
Minimum stock level:	100 rods
Re-order level:	200 rods
Delivery:	2 weeks from order
Re-order quantity:	Min. 100 and max. 500
Price:	£15.50 per rod
Location:	Main store

Goods Received		Goods Issued		Balance in stock
Date	Quantity	Date	Quantity	
			Opening stock	300
		15/1/87	100	200
17/1/87	500 ordered	17/1/87	50	150
		19/1/87	20	130
		25/1/87	50	80
		29/1/87	30	50
1/2/87	500 received			550
		1/2/87	30	520
		3/2/87	100	420

Along with many other aspects of Components Ltd., this stock control system is being computerised. It will automatically carry out all the calculations and inform the stock controller when the buffer stock level has been reached. For ease of analysis the computer can also print out the information graphically.

Task

Using the information on the stock control card (Fig. 5.8), draw up a graph of the brass rod stock from 15 January 1987 to 3 February 1987, similar to the one of Fig. 5.7. Notate your graph with the following:

(i) Delivery/procurement time.
(ii) Re-order level.
(iii) Buffer stock.
(iv) Delivery date.
(v) Re-order points.

Whilst Components Ltd. appear to have a satisfactory stock control system, other firms often experience stock problems. This is often the case when usage of a particular type of stock occurs at irregular intervals, or when deliveries are placed for varying quantities at irregular times. Unusual events may also cause stock shortages such as the processing of a rushed order when insufficient time is given to re-order stocks.

Finally, we may consider the extreme cases for very high levels of stock or very low levels of stock.

The case for high stock levels arises when a firm may be aware that shortages in a particular type of raw material or component is likely to occur. This may be due to industrial action, such as before the miners' strike in 1984/85. It was noted that both the National Coal Board and its major customers, the Central Electricity Board, had vast quantities of coal in their yards. Natural and climatic conditions might have similar effects, such as the storing of grain in anticipation of a poor harvest. The extra cash tied up in these high levels of stock can be seen as an insurance against insufficient supplies.

A similar case for high stocks occurs when inflationary pressure forces up the costs of raw materials. It is then sound business practice to purchase sizeable quantities of these materials at the present price to avoid purchasing them in a few months' time at a much inflated price.

The case for very low levels of stock, below what the cautious stock controller would advise, has come about through the 'just in time' (JIT) school of stock management. JIT is to be found in industries where highly technical types of components are needed and where there is a strong commercial link between customer and supplier. The system results in the purchasing firm being able accurately to anticipate demand and indicating its requirements at very short notice. The supplier responds, within hours, to his customers' needs.

The outcome is very low or even zero idle stock which releases cash for other purposes as well as previously used stock areas, which can now be turned into production space. Perhaps in the future JIT will become increasingly popular but many firms are hesitant to become over-reliant on one supplier for their essential materials.

Test Yourself

Using the words at the bottom of the exercise, fill in the missing spaces.

1 ...... is the means of changing raw materials into finished products.
2 The ...... is an example of the division of ......
3 ...... is often known as the first ......
4 As output increases ...... falls.
5 ...... is the production of a group of similar items in stages.
6 An insurance broker needs to be located near to his ......, or with easy ...... with them.
7 Areas of high ...... have been given the advantages of ......
8 ...... is the method of checking goods produced at various stages of manufacture.
9 Many firms have ...... stock control systems.
10 ...... is a method of stock control which depends on close links between customer and supplier.

unemployment   economist   quality control   just-in-time

unit cost   batch   computerised   production

factory system   communication   Adam Smith   labour

customers   development zones

Questions

1 Give examples of jobs where there is a high degree of specialisation.
2 What are the main advantages and disadvantages of specialisation?
3 Write a diary in the day of the production controller of Components Ltd. (see chapter for specific details).
4 What factors determine the optimal (lowest cost) level of stocks in a company?
5 Why must quality control be an important aspect of a companies production from design to delivery?

Chapter 6

Raising Capital

All businesses need to raise capital. Capital is the term given to the money used to run a business. In this chapter we shall look at both the sources of capital and some of its uses.

6.1 Start-up Capital

When a person or group of people decides to go into business for themselves they will have a limited number of ways of raising finance. They may have their own savings, kept in deposit accounts, or with a building society. They may have inherited money or perhaps received a redundancy settlement. Such sources may be sufficient for the needs of the smallest business but usually businesses require other ways of raising money.

Task

Claire Adams has recently finished studying pottery at a local college. She feels she has a talent for producing ceramics on a commercial basis.

1. List the main things she will require to set herself up in business, assuming she will sell her output to a local craft shop on a sale or return basis.
2. See if you can place an approximate value to these items and give a total.
3. Indicate which of these items need only to be purchased at the beginning of the business, and those which will need to be constantly purchased or paid for.

If a new business exhausts its own funds, then a number of institutions may be prepared to provide money, depending upon the circumstances of the business. Banks are the most common source of finance to a business. They may provide money in two main forms.

An overdraft

This will be the same sort of facility offered to a personal account customer. The client is allowed to overdraw their current (cheque account) up to an agreed limit. This arrangement allows the business to vary its indebtedness to the bank and the overdraft will fluctuate according to circumstances. The bank will charge the customer interest only on the amount outstanding. Due to the flexible nature of overdrafts they are a popular method of financing short-term requirements rather than for long-term debts.

A bank loan

Banks may be prepared to loan substantial amounts of money to an existing business with a proven record of success. Small and new businesses will find bank loans harder to come by. Banks need to safeguard their customers' investments and will not lend money to doubtful or risky ventures. Unfortunately many new businesses fall into this category. To reduce the bank's risk they may insist upon the business self-financing the majority of the money (only lending perhaps 30% of the capital).

The bank may also require security on the loan in the form of additional insurance cover, or the mortgage deeds of the owner's property. They will always want to see a business plan, which would give details about the aims and objectives of the business, the nature of the firm, other sources of finance, the research carried out to establish the nature of the market (market research), a projected balance sheet, profit and loss account and possible cash flow forecast. Even with all this information a small business may still find difficulty in persuading banks to provide finance.

Fortunately in an attempt to encourage small business ventures, the government has set up a Small Business Loan Guarantee Scheme, whereby the banks (under certain guidelines) will lend the money, whilst the government will underwrite the risks involved.

Banks will also provide an enormous range of services to businesses of all sizes other than simply loaning money. These services may include:

(i) Bank standing order — for the payment of regular bills — e.g. electricity, rates, mortgage, etc.

(ii) Deposit account — for placing money to earn interest on a long-term basis.

(iii) Current account — providing cheque and cheque guarantee facilities, overdraft, cash card (giving means of withdrawing cash 24 hours a day).

(iv) Bank statements, giving a detailed and accurate record of financial transactions carried out through bank accounts.

(v) Bank giro for transferring money from one bank account to another. This is particularly useful for transferring salary and wages between business and employee.

(vi) Safe custody of valuable documents, e.g. mortgage deeds, articles and memorandums of association.

(vii) Advice on business and personal financial matters.

(viii) Supplying foreign currency and travellers' cheques.

(ix) Bank references to suppliers.

Whilst banks are an invaluable source of a wide range of financial services, small businesses may also obtain money from finance houses (such as Mercantile Credit, Lombard North Central, UDT, etc.). These companies specialise in the granting of instalment credit facilities. These arrangements are similar to those offered to a private individual wishing to purchase an item on hire purchase (HP) arrangements. A business may wish to lease (rent) or buy a company car, commercial vehicle, land or equipment. The finance company will draw up a formal agreement, whereby the business agrees to pay a series of instalments, usually on a monthly basis over a number of years, back to the finance company. During the repayment period the business has the use of the equipment (e.g. a company vehicle) whilst being owned by the finance company. At the end of the repayment period the asset becomes the legal property of the business. Such an arrangement has the advantage of not requiring a large amount of capital to purchase the item at the beginning of its useful life. However, the finance company will charge a substantial interest payment over the loan period and such interest may also include a risk factor depending on the business' own circumstances.

New businesses may also wish to obtain credit from their suppliers. This will become a source of short-term finance, allowing the business to receive goods and use them before paying for them. Yet again new businesses will find such finance limited as suppliers often only allow credit to established customers. However, with careful negotiation and using a banker's reference many small firms are able to defer payment for several months, giving valuable breathing space to establish themselves and their products in the market.

6.2 Circulating Capital

Many new businesses find that they are restricted in the amount of capital which is available to them. If the product or service they are providing has a market then they should be in a position to begin self-financing their own activities. This is known as circulating or working capital and is the money and stocks of goods used in day-to-day trade to make a profit. Such profit can then be re-invested (or ploughed back) into the business to purchase more raw materials, which can be turned into finished goods, sold and again turned into cash. This is known as the working capital or circulating capital cycle and can be represented diagrammatically:

Fig. 6.1

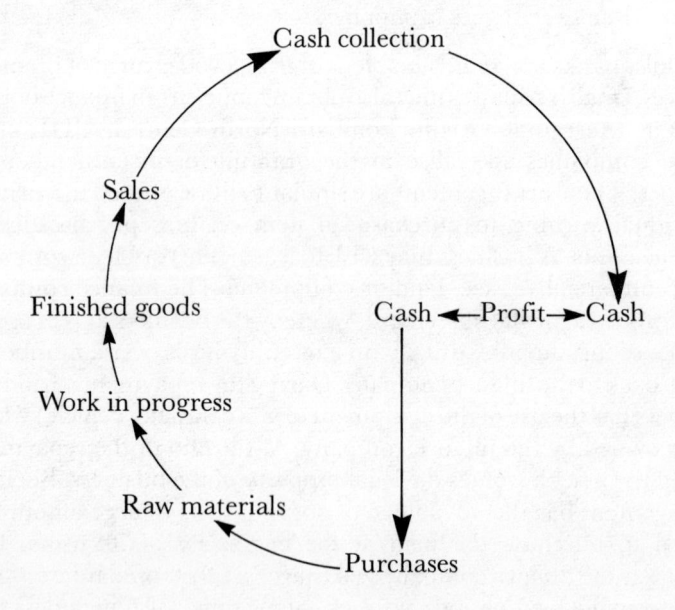

```
                Cash collection
              ↗                ↘
       Sales                     
        ↑                        
   Finished goods    Cash ← Profit → Cash
        ↑                        
   Work in progress              
        ↑                        |
    Raw materials                |
              ↖                ↙
                  Purchases
```

Task

Components Ltd. manufacture the small metal components which fit on to the back of televisions and videos. Explain, using the diagram above, the circulation of working capital from the ordering of the metal rods to the payment of goods by their customers.

To make the circulation of capital as efficient as possible a company may wish to follow a number of policies.

(i) To increase the amount of credit and length of time before it settles its debts and so reduce the requirement for cash.
(ii) Reducing the amount of money tied up in stock. By carefully examining the amount and usage of stock (stock control) a business may be able to release money which could be used more effectively elsewhere in the business.
(iii) By attempting to get payment from customers quickly can increase the amount of money available to be ploughed back into the business (credit control).

Task

How might the credit controller of a small double-glazing firm attempt to get payment from their customers quicker? You may assume that customers pay only on the satisfactory completion of a job.

6.3 Fixed Capital

Much of the start-up capital raised by a new company will be spent on the purchasing of machinery, office equipment, transport, buildings, etc. These items are not for resale but are kept to be used again and again in the course of the business. They are known as fixed assets and the money needed for their purchase is called fixed capital. Earlier in this chapter we identified a number of ways by which new business may raise such capital. We also noticed how often such capital was insufficient to meet the needs of the expanding business. As a business grows so will its requirements for larger sums of money to purchase newer equipment, to increase the amount of machinery required, to expand the premises or to build a larger factory unit. Such expansion may require thousands and sometimes millions of pounds. Re-invested profit may be a source of such capital and for many firms they need never look to outsiders to finance such growth. However, a large number of firms do need to tap the financial resources of other business institutions or private investors.

A partnership is one method of attracting additional fixed capital. A sole trader takes an additional partner, who may provide his own capital. If the new partner only wishes to invest and take his proportion of the profit without being involved in the daily running of the business, he may become a dormant or sleeping partner. Such arrangements are common where a mother or father may wish to provide a financial stake in their son or daughter's business. However, a partner has the same *unlimited liability* which a sole trader faces and could experience personal bankruptcy if the business could not pay its debts.

Many private individuals may see the advantage of investing in a business venture but be unhappy to face the consequences of unlimited liability. It is for this reason that the limited liability company exists. The capital required for the business is divided into equal parts known as *shares* which are then sold. The buyers of these shares are called *shareholders* and become collectively the owners of the business. If the business were to fail, then the shareholders would only lose the money they had paid for their shares and nothing more. Thus their liability is limited to the value of their investment.

Limited liability companies fall into two distinct types (see Chapter 2); the private limited company (Ltd.) and the public limited company (PLC). A private limited company's shares may only be sold privately and with the agreement of the other shareholders. This is often the form of business used by a small family concern which wishes to maintain control of the company. It does allow substantial amounts of capital to be raised by issuing shares on a limited liability basis, so overcoming some of the financial drawbacks of a partnership.

The circle of investors for a private company is still relatively small. It is only the public limited company which is able to sell its shares to the general public often using the market place of the Stock Exchange for the selling and buying of shares.

6.4 Shares

A shareholder puts money into a business in order to get a share of the firm's profits called a *dividend*. The dividend is the yearly distribution of profits to shareholders and will vary according to the success (or otherwise) of the business. A number of different types of share exist. The most common is the *ordinary share*. These are the main risk-bearing shares *(risk capital)* and their dividend fluctuates on an annual basis. As each ordinary share in a company is of equal value the shares are also called equities (meaning fairness or justice).

Some companies issue *preference shares* which earn a fixed dividend, e.g. 10% return on the face value of the share. They have preference over ordinary shares in that their fixed dividend is paid out before it is decided how much to pay ordinary shareholders. They also get preferential treatment if the business fails, for once all the debts have been paid any money remaining is used to repay preference shareholders before repayment is made to ordinary shareholders.

Occasionally a company may issue *cumulative preference shares*. If the full fixed dividend is not paid out in one year the holder of cumulative shares is paid any arrears in following years. The fixed dividend is then paid in addition to that owing from previous years, before payment is made to ordinary shareholders.

Example

The Southern Manufacturing Company has raised fixed capital by issuing both ordinary and preference shares as follows:

Ordinary shares — 1 000 000 shares with a nominal or face value of £1 each.
10% Preference shares — 1 000 000 shares with a nominal or face value of £1 each.
Total share capital = £2 000 000.

In its first five years of trading it records the following profit (after tax, interest and retained profit for future reinvestment) to be distributed to shareholders.

Fig. 6.2

Year	Distributed profit	Preference shareholder profit	% of dist. profit	Ordinary shareholder profit	% of dist. profit
1980	200 000	100 000	50%	100 000	50%
1981	500 000	100 000	20%	400 000	80%
1982	100 000	100 000	100%	—	0%
1983	—	—	0%	—	0%
1984	300 000				
1985	400 000				
1986	700 000				

Note: That the preference shareholders obtain their 10% return *not* on the profit but on their investment (i.e. £1 000 000) and that the ordinary shareholders get the remaining distributed profit.

Task

1 Complete the table for 1984, 1985 and 1986.
2 Recalculate the figures, assuming that the preference shares were cumulative preference shares.
3 Comment on the return of the different types of shares for the years 1980 to 1986.

6.5 Issuing Shares/Going Public

A company may require large amounts of capital to continue its expansion. It may decide that the best method of raising substantial funds is through a stock exchange quotation. This process is known as *going public* and is a process which needs careful planning and expert advice. A number of steps are involved:

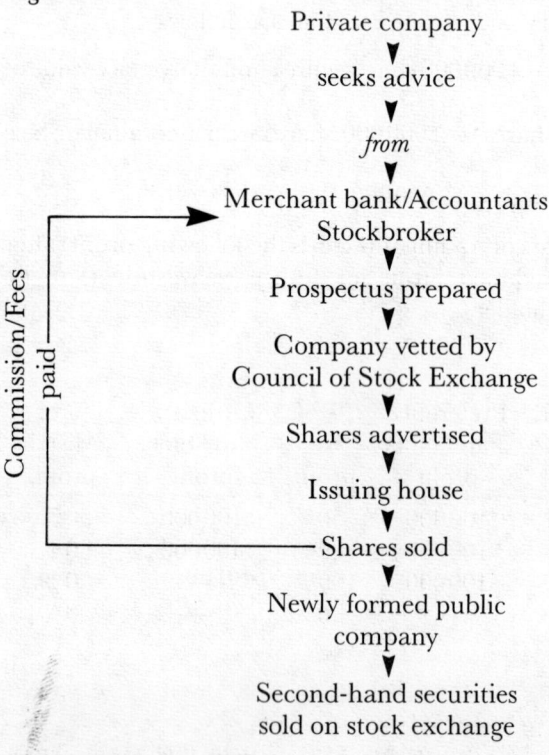

Fig. 6.3

```
                    Private company
                          ▼
                     seeks advice
                          ▼
                         from
                          ▼
              Merchant bank/Accountants
                      Stockbroker
                          ▼
                  Prospectus prepared
                          ▼
                   Company vetted by
                 Council of Stock Exchange
                          ▼
                   Shares advertised
                          ▼
                     Issuing house
                          ▼
                     Shares sold
                          ▼
                 Newly formed public
                       company
                          ▼
                 Second-hand securities
                 sold on stock exchange
```

(Commission/Fees paid — from Shares sold back to Merchant bank/Accountants/Stockbroker)

A prospectus

A prospectus is an advertisement to members of the public in respect of an issue of shares, its presentation is ruled by the council of the Stock Exchange. It would include such information as the history of the company, its recent financial results and the names of the directors.

The Council of the Stock Exchange

The council of the Stock Exchange is a body which represents members of the exchange. It is concerned with the fair dealing of member firms on the exchange.

Shares advertised

The shares will usually be advertised two weeks in advance of their issue in the financial press. It is usual to have a share application form within the advertisement.

Shares issued

Shares may be issued to the public at large at a fixed price, or placed privately with particular clients or offered for tender with no fixed price set in advance but the highest prices will be successful in obtaining shares.

Securities sold

The Stock Exchange is a secondary market for second-hand securities. In other words new share issues are not available through the Stock Exchange itself. However, due to the existence of such a secondary market it makes it much easier to raise money on the primary market (the issuing market).

6.6 The Big Bang

Since October 1986 the role of the stockbroker and stockjobber has become less well defined. The deregularisation of the Stock Exchange has also meant a number of other significant changes:

(i) Increasing computerisation of share dealings.
(ii) The commissioned charged for share trading is open to negotiation.
(iii) An opening of share dealings to a more international market.

As the fortunes of companies quoted on the Stock Exchange vary, so will their profits which will inevitably affect their dividends. As the prime motive for holding shares is to obtain a dividend on shares held, then changes in dividend will affect the demand for shares. If a dividend forecast is good then more people will wish to hold shares in that company; this will tend to push up the price.

Likewise a poor trading year for a company, the flop of one of its products, or the closing of one of its export markets will tend to cause shareholders to withdraw their money from such companies. This will increase the supply of shares available and the dealer will need to cut the price of these shares in order to sell them. Such price fluctuations give the *market price* of a share which will usually differ from the original nominal or par value of the share. It is the market price of the share which is quoted on the financial pages of the daily papers and which usually indicates the price change of shares.

The Financial Times

The overall performance of shares is monitored by *The Financial Times* through its share indexes. *The Financial Times* industrial ordinary index is an often quoted index of the leading shares from most industrial sectors. A significant movement in a large number of shares may be brought about due to exchange or interest rate charges, oil price movements, etc. Such economic factors can have a substantial impact on company fortunes and allow economic commentators to analyse their impact through such an index.

6.7 Other Methods of Raising Capital

Factoring

Increasing in popularity as a means of increasing working capital is for a firm to employ a factoring agent. The company allows the agent to handle its debt collection from customers, in return for the value of the debts less a suitable commission for administration and risk taking (e.g. bad debts and non payment). Many companies find such an arrangement very beneficial allowing specialists to handle the paperwork involved in debt collection as well as providing more immediate finance.

Debentures

A debenture is a method of raising long-term finance, usually through a bank or other financial institution. The debenture is a commitment to repay a fixed sum at a specific date (the maturity date). The commitment will involve interest payments to be made during the period of the loan, with the capital to be repaid on the maturity date. Security on the loan is usually in the form of the deeds of the company's premises or other fixed assets. If the capital sum is not repaid on the maturity date, or the company defaults on repayment, then the lender can use the debenture to secure the appropriate asset. The asset can then be sold (turned into liquid funds, i.e. cash — known as liquidation of an asset) to repay the outstanding amount.

Raising Capital

Test Yourself

Using the appropriate words from the bottom of this exercise, fill in the blank spaces in the following sentences:

1. A person's own savings may be a source of ...... capital.
2. New businesses often find ...... in raising capital.
3. An ...... is a flexible means of borrowing money from a bank.
4. Banks may give a ...... to a business' supplier to enable them to receive goods on ......
5. ...... capital is often spent on purchasing machinery, equipment and vehicles.
6. A person investing in the shares of a company expects to earn ......
7. ...... is the process by which a private limited company becomes a public limited company.
8. ...... is an indicator of the fortunes of the Stock Exchange.
9. A ...... is a specialist firm who will handle the debt collection of a business.
10. ...... are a method of raising long term finance.

reference   fixed   start-up   going public

dividends   credit   difficulty   factoring agent

overdraft   Financial Times share index   debentures

Questions

1. List four sources of short-term finance available to a business.
2. List four methods of longer-term finance available to a business.
3. Why do new companies experience difficulties in raising capital?
4. Imagine you are wishing to set up a small business and wish to seek a bank loan. How would you prepare for the interview? What information would the bank manager expect you to have?
5. What are the advantages of a private company *going public*?
6. Why does the market price of a company's shares tend to fluctuate over time?

Chapter 7
Reporting, Planning and Control

Any business, whatever its size, needs information about its financial position; whether it has made a profit or loss; whether it can pay the bills it will receive in the next few weeks; how the money it has raised was spent, and so forth. Such information allows the decision-makers of a firm to measure the success or otherwise of their policies. It also gives other people who have interests in the business a knowledge of the state of its affairs. Such interested parties would include employees, owners, suppliers, customers and the firm's own bankers.

In this chapter we shall examine the reports that companies have to prepare, as well as the methods of planning future developments and controlling costs.

Limited companies (both private and public), by law, have to prepare annual statements of their trading position. These are in the form of a balance sheet and profit and loss account. Many companies go much further and give information to shareholders, employees and other interested parties. This may include cash flow statements and detailed analyses of sales revenue.

7.1   The Balance Sheet

The aim of most businesses is to make a profit for their owners. The size of the profit will depend upon how efficiently the company has used its resources (assets). The balance sheet of a company shows the assets of the company. These are shown on the right-hand side of the balance sheet; on the left-hand side is a list showing how the company financed these assets (the liabilities). The balance sheet is drawn up at a point in time known as the year end and gives a view of the state of the company at that time.

The liabilities

The liabilities are listed in order of their currency, i.e. those at the bottom requiring earlier repayment than those at the top. Indeed the

Fig. 7.1

Example of a balance sheet (T-method)

FINHAM LTD.

BALANCE SHEET

(as at 31 March 1987)

Liabilities		Assets	
Shareholders capital:		Fixed assets:	
Shares	50 000	Land and buildings	45 000
Reserves	15 000	Machinery, fixtures and fittings	35 000
Long-term liabilities:		Vehicles	10 000
Bank loan	15 000		
Debenture	10 000	Other assets	—
Short-term liabilities:		Current assets:	
Tax due	2 000	Stock	5 000
Overdraft	3 500	Debtors	3 000
Creditors	4 500	Bank balance	1 500
		Petty cash	500
	£100 000		£100 000

shareholder funds will never be repaid (although they may change hands) unless the company goes into liquidation.

Shareholders capital is the owners' wealth tied up in the business. This is in the form of various kinds of shares (see Chapter 6) and reserves. Reserves are usually profit which has been ploughed back into the business and used to purchase assets in the business.

Long-term liabilities can come in many different forms. They are amounts borrowed by the company which are not due for repayment in the current year. The two types of long-term liabilities given in the example balance sheet are the bank loan and debenture and have been described in Chapter 6.

Short-term liabilities (or current) liabilities are amounts owed by the company, which have to be paid within twelve months. An overdraft from a bank, naturally falls within this category as it can be recalled on demand by the bank. Any amounts which have still to be paid by the business at the year end are also termed short-term liabilities and may include amounts due to suppliers for goods and services obtained on credit or unpaid taxes for profit earned in the last financial year.

The assets

Assets are listed in order of their liquidity. Liquidity is a term used to indicate the ease or speed with which an asset can be turned into cash.

Task

Consider all the things you, personally, own, including any cash, money held in a building society account, etc. Now order them so that the most liquid assets are the bottom and the least liquid at the top. This list may look something like this:

Least liquid	(a)	Luther the dog.
	(b)	Record player.
	(c)	Bicycle.
	(d)	Fifty records.
	(e)	Collection of rare coins.
Most liquid	(f)	Building society account.
	(g)	Cash.

You will notice how the money held in a building society account can be turned into cash with greater ease than a collection of rare coins and that the bicycle is an easier asset to sell than a record player. This principle of liquidity gives the order for a company's assets on the balance sheet. Thus at the top right-hand side are the least liquid assets, called *fixed assets*. These are long-term resources of a business used to provide goods and services over their life, rather than to be sold in the course of normal trading. In our example (Fig. 7.1) they would include the land and buildings of the business, machinery, fittings and vehicles owned by the business. The problem of valuing some of these assets may be difficult. How does an accountant value the land or buildings of the business when they might have been purchased many years ago? It is usual to value assets at their present market value, often using professional valuers to give as near an accurate figure as possible. Many fixed assets may lose value from year to year, such as the companies' motor vehicles. Such a loss of value is known as depreciation and companies will indicate the amount of depreciation of an asset on the balance sheet.

Example

Finham Ltd. owns two company cars at 31 March 1987. These cars are now two years old. They originally cost £8000 each. Due to depreciation their real value on the balance sheet is quoted as £10 000 rather than the £16 000 original cost.

This idea of depreciation also affects assets such as machinery and equipment which do not have a definite life-span.

Some fixed assets cannot be seen (called intangible assets) but they may appear on the balance sheet all the same. These are assets like goodwill (built up by customer loyalty and the good reputation of the company), or trademarks. As these assets are difficult to value many companies do not include them on their balance sheet.

Other assets may include the ownership of shares by one company in another company. Current assets are short-term resources, either in liquid form or expected to be used up or turned into cash within twelve months. At the top of this category are the stocks of business. These stocks may be in the form of raw materials or components, awaiting work to be carried out on them. Work-in-progress may be part-finished goods still on the factory floor awaiting completion. Finished goods are assets awaiting despatch to customers. Other types of stocks may include stationery and maintenance materials to be used up in the course of business.

The amount of stocks in a business depends on the nature of the company. For instance a large construction company may have the majority of its assets valued as stocks, e.g. part finished roads and housing estates. Other businesses dealing in perishable goods, such as vegetables, will have low stock values. The holding of stock will mean the 'tying up' of money for periods of time and this can be expensive for a business. Effective control of stock is often seen as a means of turning assets into cash as quickly as possible and so improving the profitability of the business.

Debtors are an asset owned by the company in the form of people who have purchased goods or services on credit from the business but who have yet to settle their debt. Many firms sell on a credit basis, expecting payment within 28 days of despatch of the goods. While a common business practice, it can tie up large sums of money in the form of debtors. Regrettably, some debtors may further delay payment or in a few cases not be able to make final payment (i.e. due to their having ceased to trade) and such debts became bad debts and will have to be 'written-off' the balance sheet eventually.

The most liquid assets are usually in the form of amounts kept in

Fig. 7.2

Example of a vertical or columnar balance sheet

Sources of funds

Shareholders capital:		
Shares	50000	
Reserves	15000	
		65000
Long-term liabilities:		
Bank loan	15000	
Debentures	10000	
		25000
Current liabilities:		
Tax due	2000	
Overdraft	3500	
Creditors	4500	
		10000
		£100000

Uses of funds

Fixed assets:		
Land and buildings	45000	
Machinery and fittings	35000	
Vehicles	10000	
		90000
Current assets:		
Stock	5000	
Debtors	3000	
Bank balance	1500	
Petty cash	500	
		10000
		£100000

bank accounts (current accounts) and as cash-in-hand (petty cash). Such amounts are usually kept to a minimum as they represent 'idle' funds which are not working for a business.

So far we have represented the balance sheet in its traditional or 'T' form but increasingly businesses are using a columnar (or vertical) form of presentation. This is simply a rearrangement of the balance sheet to allow easier analysis of information.

Fig. 7.2 is the Finham Ltd. balance sheet, shown vertically, for the year ended 31 March 1987.

7.2 The Profit and Loss Account

The profit and loss account is the other main financial document of a business. It shows the results of the business over a period of time (usually half-yearly or yearly) in terms of the company's profit or loss. Just as the balance sheet is divided into appropriate sections so is the profit and loss account. Fig 7.3 is the profit and loss account for

Fig. 7.3 *Example of a profit and loss account*

PROFIT AND LOSS ACCOUNT OF FINHAM LTD.
1 April 1986 to 31 March 1987

(a) Trading (operating) account	Sales revenue		80000
	Less cost of goods sold:		
	—materials	25000	
	—direct labour	20000	
	—direct overheads	10000	
			55000
	Gross profit		25000
	Less selling expenses	3000	
	administrative expenses	7000	
			10000
(b) Profit and loss account	Trading (operating) profit		15000
	Less interest		1000
	Profit before tax		14000
	Less tax		4000
			10000
(c) Appropriation account	Profit after tax		
	Profit after tax		10000
	Less ordinary dividend		5000
	Retained profit for year		£5000

Finham Ltd. for the period 1 April 1986 to 31 March 1987. (Note how the trading period usually finishes on the same date as the year end date on the balance sheet.)

The trading account

The trading account consists of revenue for sales made in the year, less operating expenses. It is usual to divide the expenses into direct costs such as materials and direct labour (i.e. those people involved directly in producing the goods or services) and indirect costs such as the office administration and secretarial support for a business along with the selling expenses (i.e. advertising and marketing of the products). The final figure on the trading account is the trading profit.

The profit and loss account

The profit and loss account starts with the trading profit and deducts interest and taxation which is paid in the year. Interest is seen as a separate cost for borrowing money for a period. Taxation usually refers to the corporation tax a company will pay to the Inland Revenue on its profits.

The appropriation account

The appropriation account shows the profit after tax for a period and how that profit was used. This will usually be in payment to shareholders in the form of dividend as a reward for their investment in the company. The remaining profit will become the funds available to the business for reinvestment (sometimes called plough-back profit).

7.3 Analysis of Accounts (Ratio Analysis)

Both the balance sheet and profit and loss accounts are important pieces of financial information, useful for a wide range of people interested in the affairs of a specific company. From these two documents much information can be gained about the strengths and weaknesses of a business. This information is usually gained by comparison of important parts of both the balance sheet and profit and loss account. Such comparison uses a variety of ratios which can be used to compare how the business is progressing from one year to the next (trend analysis) or by comparing the results of one company with another of a similar size or within the same industry or market (inter-company comparison).

Let us look at the most common types of ratios used and what they can indicate:

Profitability and efficiency ratios

(i) The prime efficiency ratio is a measure of the operating profit that has been generated from the net assets of a business. The net assets are all the assets of a business less those liabilities due for early repayment (i.e. current liabilities). Thus in the case of Finham Ltd.:

$$\text{Prime efficiency ratio} = \frac{\text{Operating profit}}{\text{Net assets}} = \frac{15\,000}{90\,000} = 0 \cdot 166$$

or as a percentage $= 16 \cdot 7\%$

(ii) Mark-up or profit margin ratio relates the operating profit to sales revenue. In Finham Ltd.:

Example

$$\text{Profit margin ratio} = \frac{\text{Operating profit}}{\text{Sales revenue}} = \frac{15\,000}{80\,000} = 0 \cdot 1875$$

or as a percentage $= 18 \cdot 75\%$

From such information the management of a business will be able to compare performance and determine how effectively the assets employed by the business are being used to generate sales and profit.

Liquidity ratios

(i) The current ratio reflects how well a company will be able to meet its short-term commitments. It is a comparison of short-term or current assets (those assets most easily turned into cash) and current liabilities (those liabilities which will require payment in the near future). As a rule of thumb, the current ratio should be between 1½ to 2. Too low a figure may indicate difficulty in paying debts and a liquidity or cash-flow problem. Too high a figure may indicate that too much money is tied up unprofitably.

Using Finham Ltd. as an example:

$$\text{Current ratio} = \frac{\text{Current assets}}{\text{Current liabilities}} = \frac{10\,000}{10\,000} = 1$$

In the case of Finham Ltd. there is the risk of future liquidity difficulties and the financial management of the business may need to consider ways of overcoming these problems (i.e. increasing funds available at their bank).

(ii) The acid test ratio is a more exact measure of liquidity, as it ignores stock from the calculation and therefore only includes the most liquid assets (i.e. cash and debtors). As a rule of thumb the acid test ratio should not be much below $1 \cdot 0$. In the case of Finham Ltd.:

$$\text{Acid test ratio} = \frac{\text{Liquid assets}}{\text{Current liabilities}} = \frac{5000}{10\,000} = 0 \cdot 5$$

Again, such a low figure would be cause for some alarm at Finham Ltd. and indicates that some form of corrective action is needed.

7.4 Management Accounts

So far we have looked at the financial statements of a business and some of the uses to which they can be put. However, most businesses require far more detailed and specific information to help guide the business on a daily basis. Such information comes in the form of management accounts. It helps to determine future policy within the company and aids decision making within the business. We shall examine two main kinds of management accounts and see how they can be used. They are budgets and cash flow accounts.

The budget

A budget is a statement prepared and agreed in advance by those responsible for it. A budget should reflect the policies to be pursued by the company. All of us have to budget in one way or another. Some people will go to the trouble of examining their income for the next month or year and comparing this with their likely expenditure. This may raise fundamental problems such as expenditure being greater than income. Such a problem can then be examined and hopefully a solution arrived at, e.g. a request for an overdraft from a bank, or to cut out that new coat which had been promised. Such personal budgeting also allows reflection on how the budget went. Did the amount of income come up to the prediction? Did we overspend? What could we have cut down upon? The principles of personal budgeting are exactly the same as those applied to business budgets. Thus budgets should be:

—realistic
—easy to understand
—the responsibility of a person or group of people
—indicating action to be taken

In business, budgets are usually allocated to each department and the department head takes the responsibility of managing and allocating his/her budget.

Thus in a large company the sales department cost budget for the next year may look like this:

Fig. 7.4

Example of a budget

COST BUDGET — SALES DEPARTMENT

1 April 1987
to
31 March 1988

Salaries	100 000
Commission	30 000
Market research	20 000
Advertising	70 000
Department overheads	30 000
	250 000

This may then be broken down into monthly or weekly budgets allowing greater depth of analysis. Such a breakdown also gives the managers more immediate feedback on how close to budget the department is performing. The feedback comes in the form of variance analysis, which simply compares the predicted budget to the actual spending. The variance can then highlight areas of weakness or overspending. Thus the sales department's monthly budget for April 1987 may look like this:

Fig. 7.5

Variance analysis

	Budget	Actual	Variance
Salaries	10 000	10 000	0
Commission	2500	2000	−500
Market research	2000	1500	−500
Advertising	8000	15 000	+7000
Department overheads	2500	2000	−500
	25 000	30 500	+5500

Immediately it can be seen that the department has overspent its budget by a considerable sum. However, we can identify that the overspending was due to the advertising expenditure in this month. The manager and those responsible for the advertising budgets now have information on which they can discuss future spending in this area. Questions will need to be answered based on whether the original budget was too low a figure, or whether the advertising was more expensive than originally planned, or whether this was extra advertising generated from a new advertising campaign. Only through sensitive budgeting can a department begin to analyse its own financial strengths and weaknesses. Budgeting allows decisions to be made based on evidence. Although much will rely on the care and involvement of those people originally drawing up the budget.

The cash flow account

A business will need to have an accurate record of the money it has available for future spending. It also needs to plan its financial needs for the future. It is no good for a firm to suddenly find that it needs an extra £15000 of income in two days' time to pay for a piece of machinery or to pay the monthly salaries. A firm needs to have its financial requirements planned weeks, if not months, in advance. Such planning allows the firm to raise extra money from a variety of sources (banks, merchant banks, finance houses, etc.) at the cheapest rate. Financial planning is greatly helped by the use of cash-flow forecasts. Rather like a budget, they make predictions about the financial future of a company. Fig. 7.6 is an example of the cash flow forecast of Ryton Ltd., a small engineering firm, as drawn up in December of the previous year.

Such a cash flow statement would be drawn up making a number of assumptions. These would include:

(i) That debtors are given credit and settle within one month of sales.
(ii) That the cash balance at the beginning of January was zero.
(iii) That other expenditures, e.g. the purchase of two machines at £10000, are to be paid in March and June.
(iv) That the information about sales and costs is accurate, based on past information and market research.

From such a cash flow statement, the financial managers of the business can identify when they will experience cash flow problems. In particular, from March through until June will require additional cash. With prior knowledge of such requirements, the company's

Fig. 7.6

Cash flow forecast

£000s	Jan	Feb	March	April	May	June	Total
Total sales	60	60	65	70	70	75	400
Cash receipts from debtors (one month on account)	45	50	50	55	60	60	320
Cash sales	10	10	10	10	10	10	60
Total cash inflow	55	60	60	65	70	70	380
Expenditure							
Labour	25	25	30	30	30	30	170
Materials	25	25	25	30	30	30	165
Overheads direct and indirect	5	5	7	7	7	7	38
Other expenditure	—	—	10	—	—	10	20
Total cash outflow	55	55	72	67	67	77	393
Total cash flow	0	+5	−12	−2	+3	−7	−13
Cumulative cash flow	0	+5	+7	−9	−6	−13	

bank may well let them have an overdraft up to a limit of £15 000, allowing flexibility over this period of time. Cash flow forecasts are therefore a method of planning — avoiding the need for 'crisis' management. Increasingly, banks and other lenders of cash will expect both new and established businesses to produce projected cash flow statements before considering loaning substantial sums of money.

7.5 Making a Profit

So far in this chapter we have looked at how a business may report and plan the financial side of the concern. We shall now look more closely at two major components of financial management — *revenue* and *costs*, and identify what exactly profit is. Most private sector organisations exist to make profit. Economists would go further and assume all firms are profit maximisers. Whatever our own views on economic or business matters, it is apparent that profit is a key concept and an understanding of it will help to gain an insight into what makes businesses successful or not.

As a simple statement, profit equals revenue minus costs.

$$\text{Profit (loss)} = \text{Revenue} - \text{Costs}$$

From such simplicity we need to examine what determines the two key components of the equation: revenue and costs.

Revenue

Revenue (sometimes called sales revenue, turnover, sales or income of a business) is a firm's trading income for a period from selling its products or services. Its simple calculation is from the equation.

$$\text{Revenue} = \text{Price} \times \text{Quantity}$$

We take as an example Leasowes Ltd., a company producing and selling tubular roof racks to garages and motoring wholesalers. If the selling price is £15, then we can plot the revenue on a graph, using the vertical axis to represent revenue and the horizontal axis to represent output and sales.

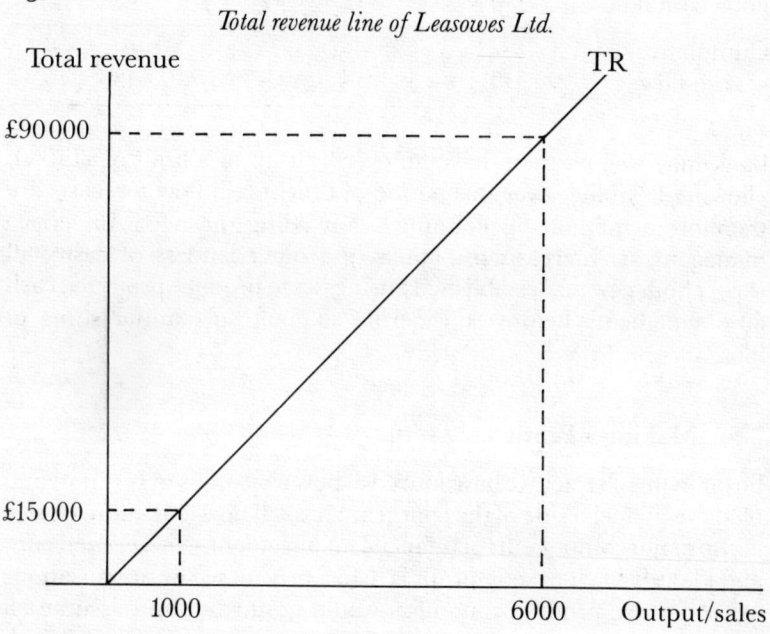

Fig. 7.7

Total revenue line of Leasowes Ltd.

Costs

Costs can be defined as expenses incurred by a company in order to produce revenue. For our purposes costs can be divided into two types — fixed and variable. Thus the total costs of a business are made up of the total fixed costs and the total variable costs of a business.

Total costs = Total fixed costs + Total variable costs

Let us now see what makes up these two different types of costs:

Fixed costs are the costs that a business has to pay for, irrespective of the output of the firm. These costs are often known as overheads, and in the case of a business like Leasowes Ltd., they would include:

the rent of the factory space	£5000 p.a.
the rates paid to the local authority	£1000 p.a.
the wages of secretarial staff and administrative staff	£20 000 p.a.
the cost of advertising the firm's products	£4000 p.a.
Total fixed costs	£30 000 p.a.

It can be seen that such costs have to be met, irrespective of how well the business is doing. If fixed costs were plotted using similar axes to those of the total revenue graph then costs would be represented by a horizontal straight line at the £30 000 level.

Fig. 7.8

Fixed costs

Revenue
Costs

£30 000
_____ Total fixed costs

_____ Output

It is often useful to know how much the fixed cost per item of output is. This will help in the pricing of the product. This is calculated by dividing the total fixed costs by the sales output. Thus:

$$\text{Unit fixed cost (average fixed cost)} = \frac{\text{Total fixed costs}}{\text{Output}}$$

Thus if Leasowes Ltd. sell 10 000 roof racks in a year then the unit fixed cost:

$$= \frac{£30\,000}{10\,000} = £3 \text{ per item.}$$

Variable costs

Variable costs are those costs which will increase as the output of the business increases. In Leasowes Ltd. these costs would include the tubular pipes used in the construction of the roof racks (£5 per rack), the fitments, e.g. the screws, rubber mountings, etc. (£1 per rack), the direct labour involved in making each rack, e.g. the bending and assembling of the rack (£3 per rack), and the packaging and transport of the racks (£1 per rack). By adding these variable costs together we arrive at a unit variable cost, which in this case is £10 per rack. As with other parts of our revenue and cost equations we can plot this information on a similar graph:

Fig. 7.9

Total variable costs

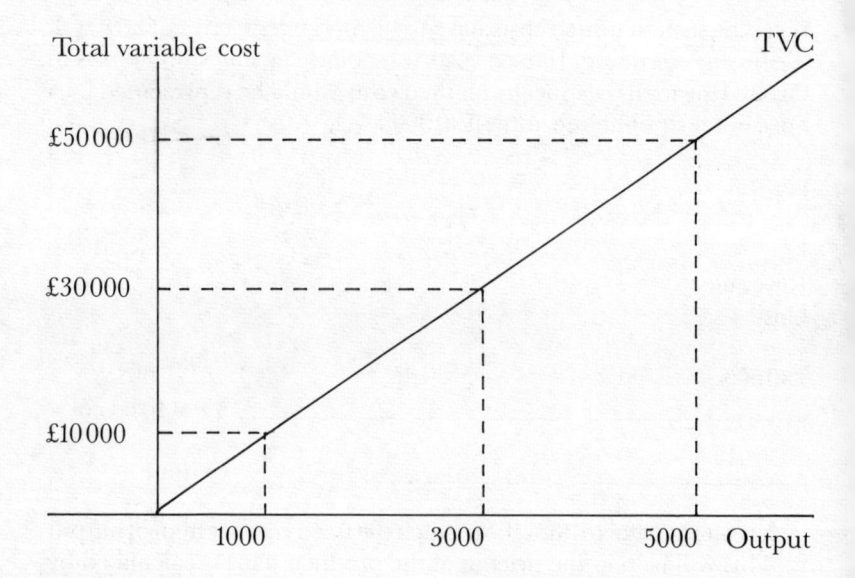

To find the total variable costs we multiply the unit (average) variable cost, by the output and plot this on the graph. Thus if output is 1000 racks, total variable costs (TVC) equals 1000 × £10 = £10 000.

Fig. 7.10

Total fixed and variable costs

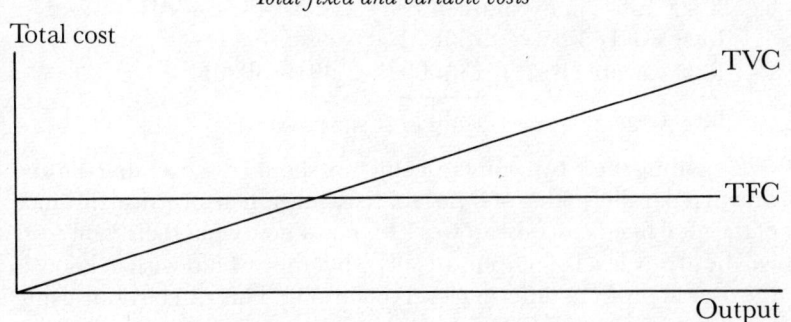

We can now bring these two types of cost together to give the total cost of running the business at various levels of output. Remembering that total costs equal total fixed costs plus total variable costs.

If we now select a number of different output levels we can determine a total cost line. If the firm makes 1000 units in a year then:

Total fixed costs	= £30 000
Total variable costs	= £10 000 (i.e. £10 × 1000)
Total costs	£40 000

Fig. 7.11

Total costs

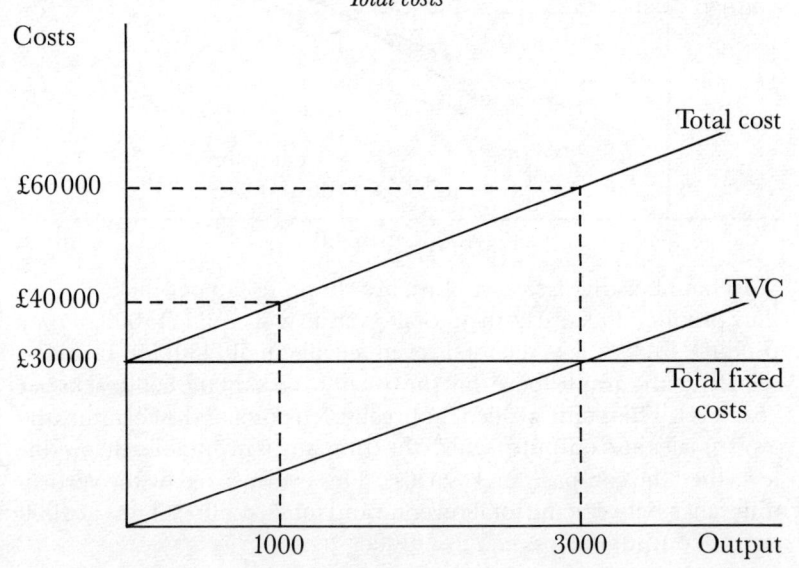

If we select another level of output

e.g. 30 000 racks per year, then
Total fixed costs =	£30 000
Total variable cost =	£30 000 (i.e. £10 × 3000)
Total costs	£60 000

By joining these two points together we should discover that the line drawn is parallel to the total variable cost line but at a vertical distance of the total fixed costs. Leasowes Ltd. now know what their total costs will be at any level of output. Ideally what they would wish to know is the overall profit at differing levels of output. This can be done using break-even analysis. It involves taking the total cost line and superimposing it upon the total revenue line, which we have drawn earlier.

Fig. 7.12

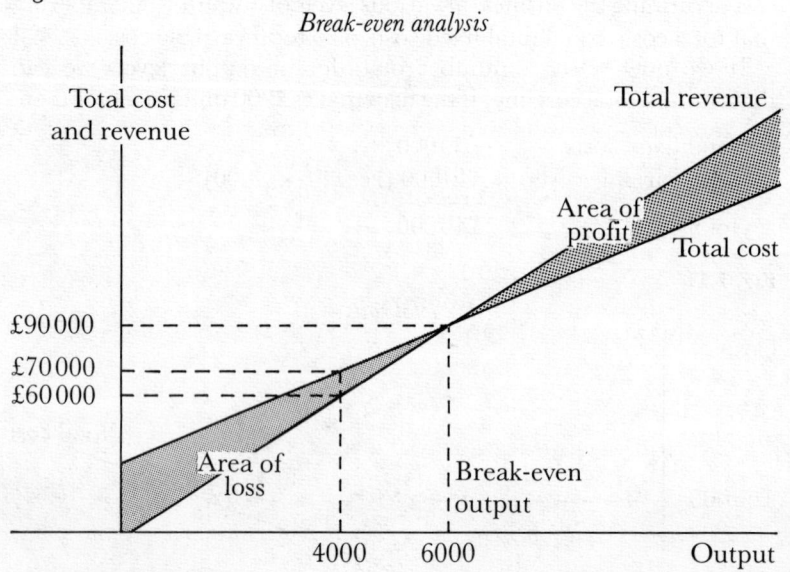

Break-even analysis

Remember that Leasowes Ltd. are charging £15 per rack. Thus if they produce 1000 racks then total revenue will equal £15 000, if they produce 10 000 racks the total revenue will equal £150 000. It can be seen from the graph above that the two lines cross at the 6000 racks per year level. This point is called the break-even point and determines the level of sales and output at which the company is profitable. Below this level then the company makes a loss. This is measured by the vertical difference between the total revenue and total cost line. Thus at 4000 units of output the loss equals £10 000.

This can, of course, be worked out mathematically by using our first equation.

Profit (loss) = Total revenue − Total costs

Thus at 4000 units

Total revenue = 4000 + £15 = £60 000

Total costs = £30 000 + (4000 × £10)
               (Total   (Total
               fixed   variable
               costs)   costs)

            = £70 000

Loss   = £60 000 − £70 000
        = £10 000

Example

If the sales-force from market research think they can sell 8000 units at this price (£15), then the profit will equal £10 000.

Again mathematically this can be calculated as follows:

Total revenue = 8000 × £15 = £120 000
Total costs   = £30 000 + (8000 × £10)
              = £110 000
Profit   = £120 000 − £110 000
              = £10 000

It can be seen how useful break-even analysis is to a business. It clearly indicates the level of output needed to achieve profit. Further to this, it gives the company definite information about their own objectives. Thus if the management of Leasowes Ltd. sees that an appropriate level of profit for the business is £10 000, then they know immediately what both their production and sales department have to do to meet this objective, i.e. to produce and sell 8000 roof racks in the coming year. Indeed break-even analysis can be a useful starting point for determining departmental budgets. In this case the production manager knows that to meet the overall objectives of the business he must keep his production costs to £10 per roof rack.

Break-even charts can also be used to show how a change in price of costs (fixed or variable) may affect profit or the break-even point. Thus the employment of another part-time office worker may push the total fixed cost up by an additional £5000 per year.

Test Yourself

Using the appropriate words from the bottom of this exercise, fill in the blank spaces in the following sentences:

1. Private and public companies have to prepare a yearly ...... and ......
2. ...... are what a company owns.
3. A balance sheet is drawn up to give a financial picture of a company's ......
4. ...... are amounts owing by a company which will have to be paid within 12 months.
5. ...... is the term used to describe the speed an asset can be turned into cash.
6. Stock, debtors and cash are examples of ......
7. ...... shows the outcome of a business' trading activities over a period of time.
8. ...... allows a firm to compare two pieces of information at one instance.
9. A ...... and a ...... are types of management accounts.
10. ...... tells a firm at what level of output the company is likely to be profitable.

break-even analysis   at a point in time   current liabilities

ratio analysis   cash flow forecast   balance sheet   liquidity

profit and loss account   owns   current assets   budget

Questions

1. List the main kinds of financial and management accounts kept by a business.
2. Who are the 'interested parties' in a company's financial records? What sort of information do they require?
3. What do you consider to be the major difficulties associated with preparing the balance sheet and profit and loss account of a company?
4. What are the essential differences between the financial accounts of a business and the management accounts of a business?
5. What is profit? Why is profit so important to a business?
6. Using graph paper and showing the calculations involved find the new break-even point for Leasowes Ltd, given the following information:

    (i) Leasowes Ltd. decide to take on a part-time office worker at £5000 per annum.
    (ii) The cost of tubular piping increases by £2 per roof rack.
    (iii) The marketing manager decides on a £5 increase in price to cover these additional costs.

PART III

PEOPLE AND WORK

Chapter 8

Human Needs and Work

A working adult spends nearly half of his/her waking hours at work. For most people their job is the only source of income and their standard of living depends upon it. However, people have very different attitudes towards their work. In this chapter we shall look at the reasons people work and the satisfaction that can be gained from it.

8.1 Why People Work

Let us look at three people and examine the reasons why they work.

(a) *Richard Haydn* is 30 years old, married with three children under the age of 5. He left school at 16 having gained a number of high CSE passes and was employed by a large engineering firm, making car components. After a 5-year apprenticeship as a technician he became a skilled fitter. He has stayed with the same company since this time, although he could have found a better paid job with another firm nearby. He enjoys his work and seeing the output of his labour. He works for 39 hours a week, and usually turns down the chance of overtime, preferring to spend the time with his growing family. He receives 20 days paid holiday a year. Last year he took the family camping in Wales. He is a member of the works social committee and plays in the company's darts and football teams. Most of his close friends are workmates or neighbours. Last year he was asked by the production manager if he would apply for a foreman's job which had became vacant but he decided against it and said '. . . the extra cash is not worth the hassle'. When asked what satisfaction he found in his job he said 'It's a good atmosphere and I've worked with my mates for a long time now. The company has a full order book and there is no chance of redundancies at the present time. This company looks after its employees and we've not had a strike since I've been here. Mind you, sometimes I do get fed up being inside all the time. The smell of oil really gets to you after a while; but overall I'm doing all right, we've got a nice house and a decent standard of living.'

(b) *Rosemary French* works from home as a child-minder: she looks after two small children, brothers, whose parents are both teachers. Her day is very ordered. The children arrive at 8.00 am and are picked up at 4.30 pm. During the day the children play or go shopping, three days a week they go to a 'minders and toddlers session' arranged by a group of local child-minders. Rosemary cooks a midday meal for them. The youngest child is still in nappies and needs changing at least twice a day. She loves working with children; her own children are now at school. She is paid £55 per week from which she buys nappies, food and pays for the 'minders and toddlers session'. She says 'The money isn't very much. If I think of it on an hourly basis I suppose I wouldn't do it. I could earn much more packing the shelves in a local supermarket but these are two lovely kids and their day works around what I have to do at home. It seems an ideal arrangement for me and I've done this for the last 5 years. When these two are of school age I'll be looking for some more.'

(c) *Paul Harrison* left university with an Honours Degree in Biology. He joined a pharmaceutical wholesaler, who later went out of business and Paul was made redundant four years ago. Since this time he has been working as a representative for two medical suppliers. He is paid a basic wage, which he admits is not very high. He makes up the rest of his income by gaining commission, based upon the amount he sells each month. He has a number of 'fringe' benefits, including a company car, an excellent pension scheme and private medical insurance. Unfortunately he does not enjoy his work. He says 'I spend a lot of time on my own, driving from one appointment to the next; it can be very lonely. Often I make a presentation to a group of doctors and know that they aren't really interested in the products. Sometimes I am expected to 'wine and dine' people; nothing wrong with that, except that I may not have a lot in common with them. But I try to keep the smile and charm going in the hope of placing an order — it can be so frustrating!' When asked why he doesn't find another job he admits 'I'm trapped really, I haven't enough experience to go into sales management. I could get another similar job to this one but that's not the answer. I'm not even sure that I like selling. If I were to get out, it would have to be a drastic change of career — some kind of retraining — perhaps even becoming a student again but that would be difficult, because I've become used to the money, the car and all that goes with the job.'

From these three case studies, we can see a number of very different reasons why people work and also some of the satisfactions and frustrations that come from working. A list of reasons for Richard, Rosemary and Paul working may include:

(i) To earn income and maintain a comfortable standard of living.
(ii) Friendship with workmates.
(iii) Easiness of job.
(iv) Conditions of work, flexible hours, holidays, benefits.
(v) Independence and lack of supervision.
(vi) Contact with people.
(vii) Job security.
(viii) Sense of purpose, the feeling of doing something useful and important.

Task

See if you can match these eight motivations for work with the three case studies.

Of course there are many other reasons for working; these may include:

(ix) Chances of promotion.
(x) The challenge of doing a difficult job.
(xi) Excitement.
(xii) Responsibility.
(xiii) Feelings of importance or power.
(xiv) Enjoyment of working out of doors.

The list is endless. Every job combines different points from those mentioned above.

Task

Consider the following jobs/careers and see which factors, from the list, apply to them. Add your own observations as well:

—Social worker.
—Production-line worker in a car plant.
—Computer programmer.
—Teacher.
—Self-employed plumber.
—Fisherman.

8.2 Work and Motivation

A number of theories exist about the question of work and motivation. These theories have been developed since the beginning of this century, with the development of the science of human behaviour and in particular the management sciences. Especially the works of F. W. Taylor, Elton Mayo, Abraham Maslow, Douglas McGregor and Frederick Herzberg can be examined to see the way that the management of people has developed.

(a) *F. W. Taylor* based his theories on the principle that work was simply to do with economic needs. The view of the worker, current in the nineteenth century and fostered by Taylor at the turn of the century, was that he simply worked for money. Taylor held the extreme view that workers were, by nature, lazy but eager to make money. Not surprisingly, his advice to managers was based upon monetary rewards. Tasks should be simple with clear quotas and incentives. Work should be closely supervised. Obviously such a view of work led to workers seeing themselves as nothing more than an extension of the machines they were operating. Such a low status view of their work often resulted in conflict and disagreement between workers and management.

(b) *Elton Mayo* was an ex-assistant of F. W. Taylor, who could see many shortcomings of the Taylor approach. Mayo's work was carried out at the Hawthorne Works of the General Electric Company in Chicago, USA during the 1920s and 1930s. He was investigating how lighting levels affected the assembly rate and quality of electrical goods. He noted how better lighting improved output but was also surprised that output also increased for the control group as well. Indeed, any change in lighting seemed to affect output. After much thought Mayo realised that it was not the amount of light available which changed production but simply that supervisors and managers were taking a personal interest in the workers. They were being seen as both useful and important.

Mayo's work led to a school of management science known as the human relations school. From his leadership managers saw that the real meaning of work lies in people's attitudes and relationships, of interest, respect, fellowship and personal freedom in their job.

(c) *Abraham Maslow* viewed the motivation for work in the form of differing levels of needs, known more formally as a hierarchy of needs. His was a relatively simple model which noted that once a person's basic or physiological needs are met (i.e. food, sleep, shelter, clothing and avoidance of pain), then a person will be motivated to move to a higher level of needs. These may be social needs of wishing to belong, to receive affection, to gain respect from others, etc. Finally the highest level of needs were the personal needs of self-fulfilment and self-esteem. This model of human behaviour can be used to explain why many people are prepared to do jobs or move into careers where the pay may not be excellent, yet provides a reasonable standard of living, but where the extra rewards in such jobs are enormous.

Fig. 8.1
A diagram to illustrate the level of human needs (after Abraham Maslow):

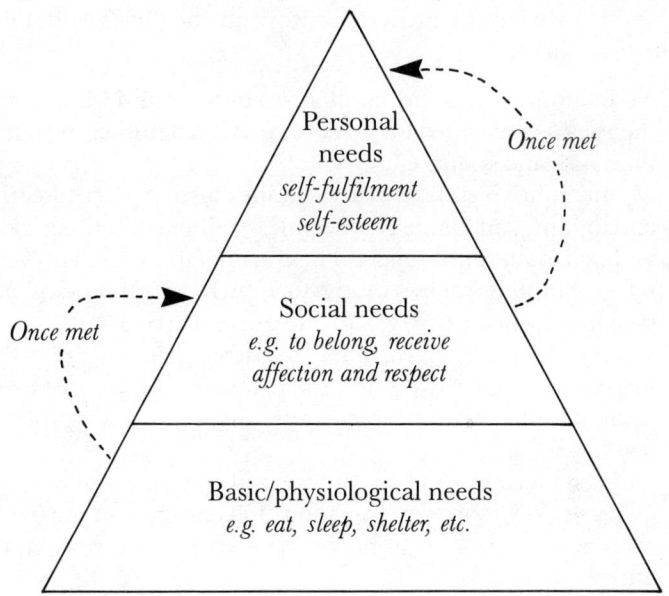

```
                    /\
                   /  \
                  / Personal \
                 /   needs    \      Once met
                / self-fulfilment\
               /   self-esteem    \
              /_____\
             /                      \
            /     Social needs       \
           /   e.g. to belong, receive \
   Once met/    affection and respect    \
          /_____\
         /                                \
        /     Basic/physiological needs    \
       /       e.g. eat, sleep, shelter, etc.\
      /_____\
```

Maslow's Scheme can also be used to explain why, when a person is driven predominantly by a hunger for a basic need then social relationships may deteriorate markedly. Thus a person on a low income who is struggling to make ends meet, may place little value upon the social relationships which may develop at his place of work but be more concerned with the level and amount of overtime available.

(d) *Douglas McGregor* was to use Maslow's approach and apply it to business management. McGregor's work is famous for his comparison of Theory X and Theory Y.

Theory X is based, essentially, on a Taylor-like person who is lazy and dislikes work. He is selfish, avoids responsibility and has no ambition. Accordingly he has to be controlled and directed by management. The blame for a company's poor performance can be seen as that of the workers.

Theory Y views a worker as someone who can enjoy work and who will seek out and take responsibility. He possesses imagination, creativity and specialist job knowledge. Suitably motivated he can be used as a decision maker, prepared to set and meet personal and organisational objectives. Management is at fault if it does not allow this to happen by co-operation and participation.

(e) *Frederick Herzberg* was to take the work of Maslow and McGregor and give it further refinement. His work in the 1950s and 1960s identified two factors:

(i) Motivators — these are similar to Maslow's and McGregor's theories, i.e. the need for achievement, recognition, responsibility, advancement, etc.

(ii) Maintenance factors, which are things such as proper heating and lighting, adequate rest facilities, well-lit conditions, clean and well maintained toilets. These are not motivators in themselves but they allow motivators such as promotion and incentive schemes to work. Herzberg carried out a large volume of research in various countries and he concluded that motivation factors were the main source of job satisfaction while maintenance factors were the main cause of job dissatisfaction.

From Herzberg's work comes the idea of job enrichment as being the key to work motivation. Job enrichment means re-shaping the job so as to maximise achievement, recognition and responsibility.

An excellent example of the application of Herzberg's work came from the design of the Volvo car plant in 1974 at Kalmar in Sweden. At this plant the workforce was divided into groups of about twenty workers. Each group completed one major stage in the production process, e.g. one group might build up the gear boxes, another the engine.

The Kalmar buildings were made up of a collection of production bays, with parts and components moving from one bay to bay by a series of electronic trolleys. Workers changed tasks regularly, discussed how work was to be organised and could transfer from one work unit to another to experience different kinds of work. Each team had its own area, which was large enough to house its own entrance, coffee area, assembly area and changing rooms. The costs of building the Kalmar factory were 10% higher than the costs of a conventional car plant, yet Volvo have noticed:

(i) A development of team spirit, involving a pride taken in the cars produced.
(ii) Greater levels of satisfaction reported from the workforce.
(iii) High standards of workmanship, giving better cars of higher quality. One of Volvo's main marketing points is the reliability of their vehicles which has boosted both the company's reputation and sales.
(iv) Less absenteeism of workers.
(v) Fewer industrial disputes.
(vi) Little difficulty in recruiting well-qualified labour.

Such an application of Herzberg's theories and those of the early management scientists can be seen in the Kalmar plant. Yet Volvo's motives were strictly economic — the company expecting to produce more cars, more efficiently, and more cheaply, consequently selling in greater volume and making more profit.

8.3 Job Enrichment

Job enrichment is a feature of many companies' policies towards factory design and man management. The advantages are for all to see: computer technology has added a new dimension to job enrichment by eliminating many of the traditionally dull, boring jobs found both on the factory floor or in the offices. Of course, it has its social cost with the destruction of many unskilled or semi-skilled jobs which were once available. Indeed some of the unemployment problems of western industrialised economies in the 1980s can be attributed to the use of new technologies replacing the older forms of traditional employment. It is, however, important to see that job enrichment is a separate issue from new technology, albeit that often they go hand-in-hand.

8.4 Pay

The monetary rewards for work: the income earned by someone in employment can be made up in a number of different ways.

Salary

A salary is a fixed sum of money usually paid each month. Salaries are paid to professional people: managers, teachers, engineers, etc.

Salaried employees are often expected to work a flexible number of hours. This means that if a job needs to be done by the end of the week then the person will work to this end, even if it means a ten or twelve hour day. Salaried staff do not expected to be paid for overtime.

Wages

Wages are paid, usually on a weekly basis for direct production workers or clerical workers in offices.

Wages are paid, usually, on the basis of the number of hours worked (time rate) or on the amount of work done (piece rate).

Time rate

Time rate involves a basic pay for a set number of hours worked, e.g. 37½ hours. Additional overtime, which is voluntary, is worked at the basic hourly rate plus an extra third or half, or even double the basic pay. In many industries overtime is used to compensate for the low basic wage. Overtime often depends upon a full order-book and when the firm is going through a lean period then overtime will be cut before redundancies are made. The result can be a substantial drop in take-home pay.

Time rate payment requires a clocking-in system at the factory gate and involves a wages department geared to often complicated calculations. Increasingly wages are worked out using computers.

Piece rate

Piece rate comes in a variety of forms. The idea behind such methods of payment is the notion that the primary motivation for work comes from money. This goes back to the work of Taylor, but piece rate is still used in many industries.

The simple piecework payment system is one based entirely upon the individual worker's output. The amount of effort is directly rewarded by additional earnings.

Such a system is rare in manufacturing industries but it is often the basis for commission paid to representatives. As an example, many double-glazing representatives earn income based entirely on the volume they sell. Thus for every £100 worth of sales made, the representative earns £15. If in a week he makes no sales, or takes a holiday, then his earnings are zero. Surprisingly this is the same principle on which dentists work, being paid on the number of treatments made.

Fig. 8.2

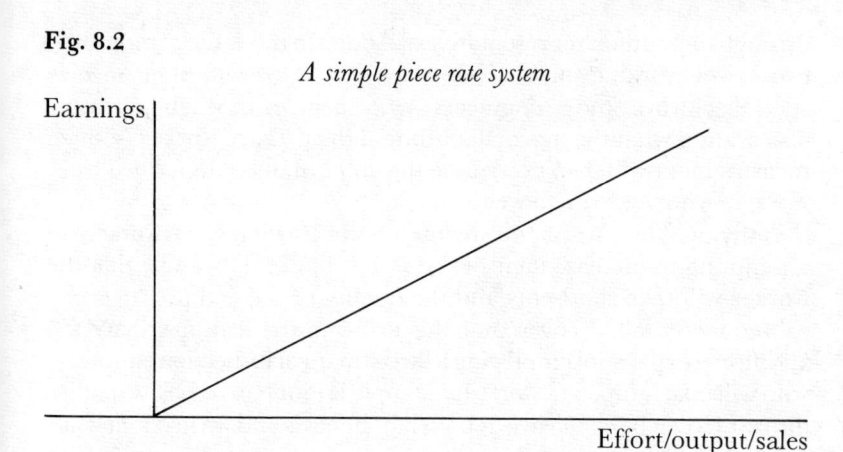

A simple piece rate system

Earnings

Effort/output/sales

Such a system provides little security of income and more common is a piece-work system with a basic element.

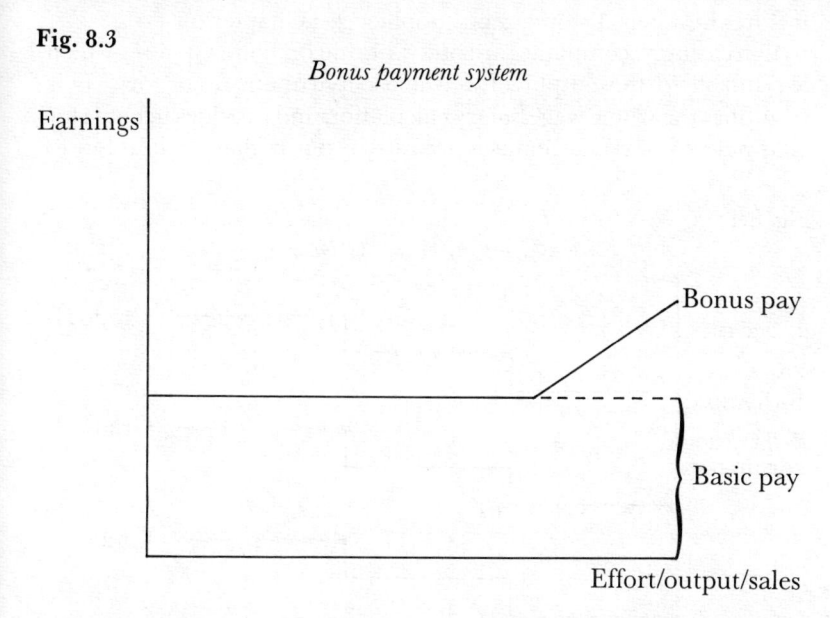

Fig. 8.3

Bonus payment system

Earnings

Bonus pay

Basic pay

Effort/output/sales

In this system the employee is guaranteed a minimum payment (see Paul Harrison — case study) but additional pay comes from exceeding a certain level of effort. Such a system is assumed to provide the motivation for harder work. Such methods of bonus pay will require a complicated wages calculation system, geared to measure the work rate of each employee. The level of bonuses will involve detailed negotiation between management and workers (usually through their union representatives). Added to this is the complicated process of working out the bonus system. This will often involve specialist work-study engineers who decide through scientific observation what the 'normal' output of the average worker is. Such measurement will then determine the amount of bonus earned from workers who perform above the norm.

Individual bonus systems, by their nature, will involve workers in attempting to increase their own output. The result can be that the worker will take short-cuts and the quality of the end product may subsequently fall. To overcome this problem the firm may have the additional expense of employing a larger team of inspection engineers who will take samples of work. If a sample is found to be below quality the results can be expensive as both labour costs and wasted materials will have to be paid for. Even worse is for a poor quality product to arrive at the final customer who will have the annoyance of returning the goods. This waste of time and money can result in ill-will and bad feelings between customer and supplier (see Chapter 5).

Increasingly, companies are now working on bonus systems which are linked to the output of a whole department or factory. This simplifies the whole wage/salary calculation and provides benefits for all grades of workers. Bonuses are related not to daily output but to

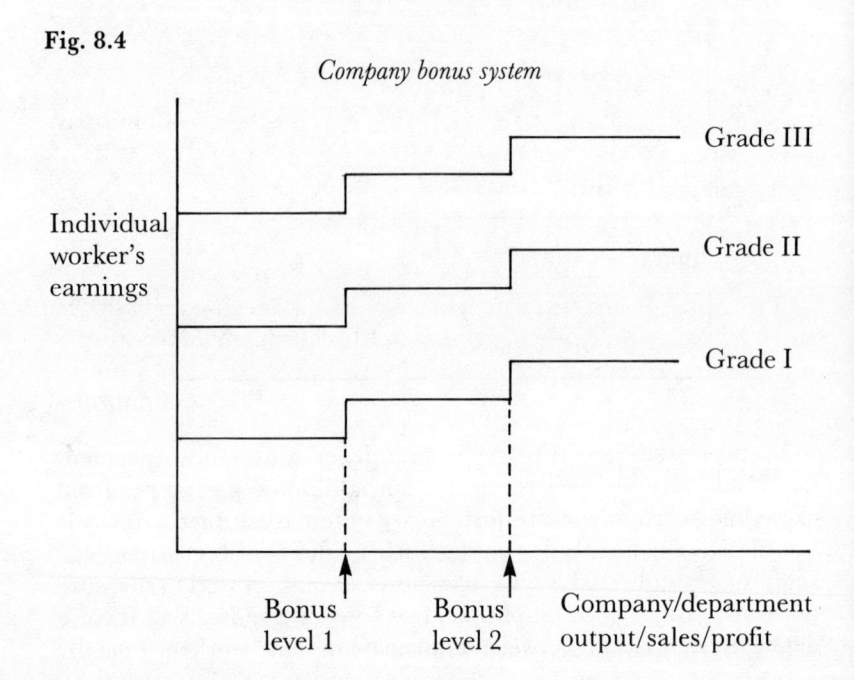

Fig. 8.4

Company bonus system

profit or sales of the whole firm. Such bonus can be paid either monthly or yearly. They also provide the additional advantage of making the individual worker feel part of a team, working for the collective good of the business as well as giving direct monetary rewards for the worker.

Company bonus system pay structure

Such systems allow the management to provide an incentive scheme for which they have greater control and the costs of which can be calculated more accurately than individual bonus systems.

Fringe benefits

Fringe benefits are becoming increasingly popular as a means of giving non-monetary benefits to employees. It is evident when looking through job advertisements in the daily papers that employers often offer a 'package' of benefits, which can be of enormous personal value to individual employees. Listed below are some of the most common fringe benefits:

(i) The company car or car user's allowance.
(ii) Removal expenses.
(iii) London (or city) allowances to compensate for the higher living costs in such areas.
(iv) Private medical insurance.
(v) Subsidised or free lunches.
(vi) Public transport allowances.
(vii) Cheap mortgages (particularly popular with banks, building societies and insurance companies).
(viii) Company housing.

The great advantage of such benefits is that they are usually tax free. Often these benefits may provide the inducement for a person to move from one company to another, even though the salaries offered may be similar.

8.5 Why Incomes Differ

Why is it that a doctor earns far more than a nurse? Why is a coal miner's wage far greater than that of a bus driver? Why is a teacher paid less than a police inspector? To answer these questions we need to understand the principles of the labour market. This brings together the two factors of the demand for labour and the supply of labour. It is the interaction between these two factors which can determine the price paid (wage or salary) for a person's work.

If we look at the demand for labour we can see that it is related to the amount paid. So the more a company has to pay for its labour then the fewer the number of people it will be able to employ. This gives us a downward sloping demand curve:

Fig. 8.5

Demand for labour 1

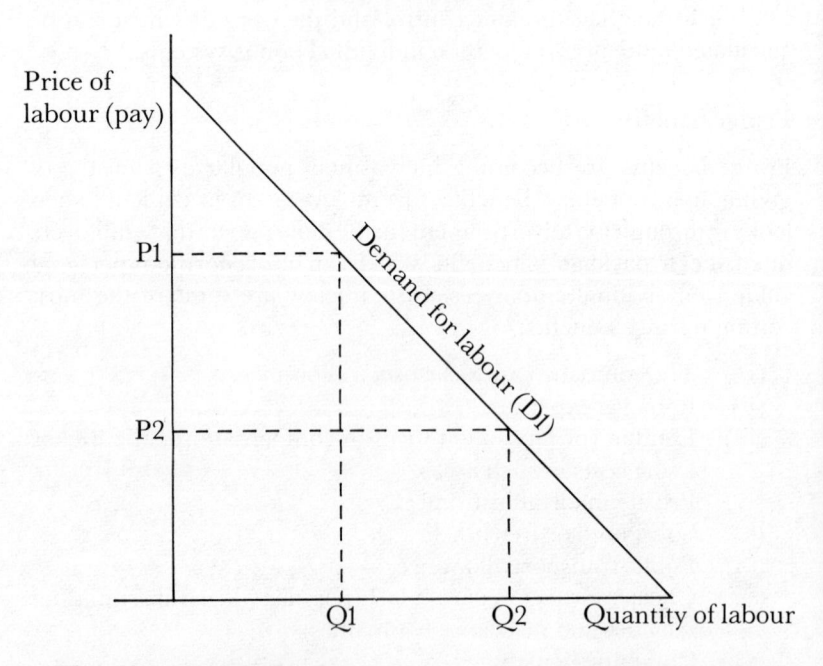

Thus if pay is high (P1) then numbers employed will be low (Q1). If the pay per employeee is low (P2) then a company may be prepared to take on more labour (Q2).

A number of factors will influence this line. For instance if the firm experiences an increase in the demand for its products then the line will move upwards and to the right (see Fig. 8.6).

Thus a company will be prepared to take on more labour and be prepared to pay more for its labour (thus moving the demand curve from D I → DII). Likewise if the demand for a company's products drops, then the demand curve for labour moves downwards and to the left. The demand for labour being derived from the final demand for the product.

Fig. 8.6

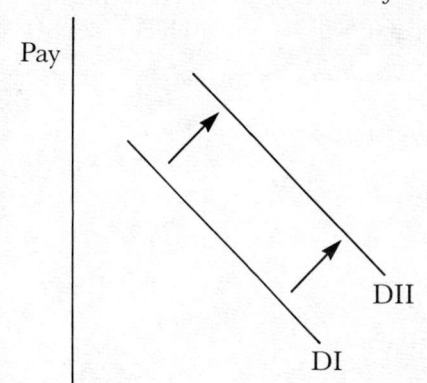

Demand for labour 2

[Graph showing Pay on vertical axis and Quantity of labour on horizontal axis, with two downward-sloping parallel lines labelled DI and DII, with arrows pointing from DI up to DII]

The supply curve for labour is also related to the price paid but in this case the line slopes upwards to the right:

Fig. 8.7

Supply of labour 1

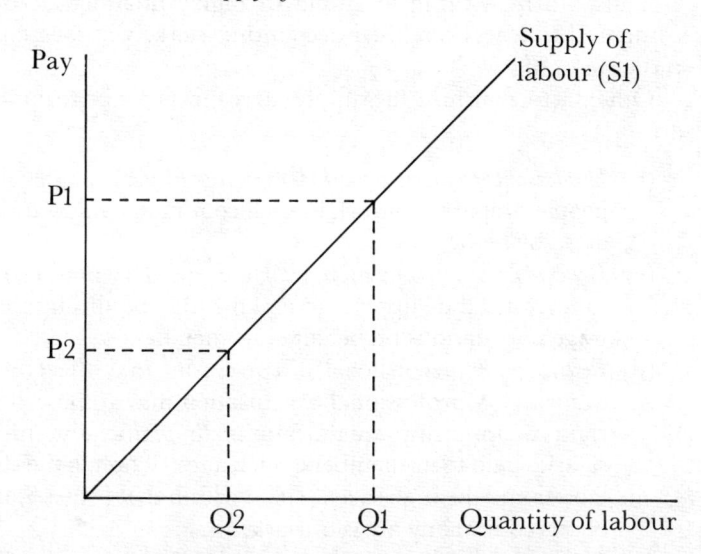

[Graph showing Pay on vertical axis and Quantity of labour on horizontal axis, with an upward-sloping line labelled Supply of labour (S1). Dashed lines indicate P1 corresponding to Q1, and P2 corresponding to Q2.]

If a firm was prepared to pay a high rate of pay (P1), then the supply of labour available would also be high (Q1). If the company were only prepared to pay a low wage (P2) then the number of people attracted to such pay would also be low (Q2).

A number of factors affect the supply line (curve).

(a) *Skills* — if the work involves a high degree of skill, or long training then the supply curve will be much higher, i.e. SII rather than SI.

Fig. 8.8

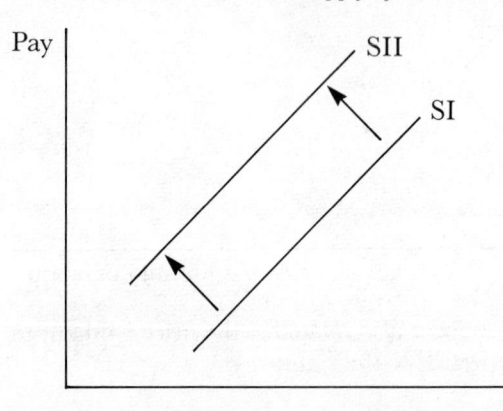

Supply of labour 2

Thus a firm wishing to employ a highly qualified accountant, compared to a less qualified accounting clerk, will face curve SII rather than SI.

Other factors pushing the supply curve upwards and to the left (SII) are:

(b) *Unpleasant or dangerous work* is often more highly paid, with fewer people prepared to work in such conditions unless induced to do so by higher wages.
(c) *Power of unions* in a particular firm or industry may also be able to force up the supply curve. This may be through effective wage negotiations on behalf of its members.
(d) *Restrictive practices* on behalf of a profession may affect the supply available. A professional organisation may impose strict and rigid membership qualifications to artificially inflate the salaries paid to its members. Such a restriction to the supply of labour and the high salaries paid within that profession can be observed in many areas of work.
(e) *Uniqueness of the individual* may explain the high earnings commanded by pop stars, footballers, etc. Their supply curve is both high and almost vertical implying an unresponsiveness of pay to the number of people available.

By combining the demand and supply curve together for a particular type of employment, we can arrive at the wage paid in this labour market.

Fig. 8.9

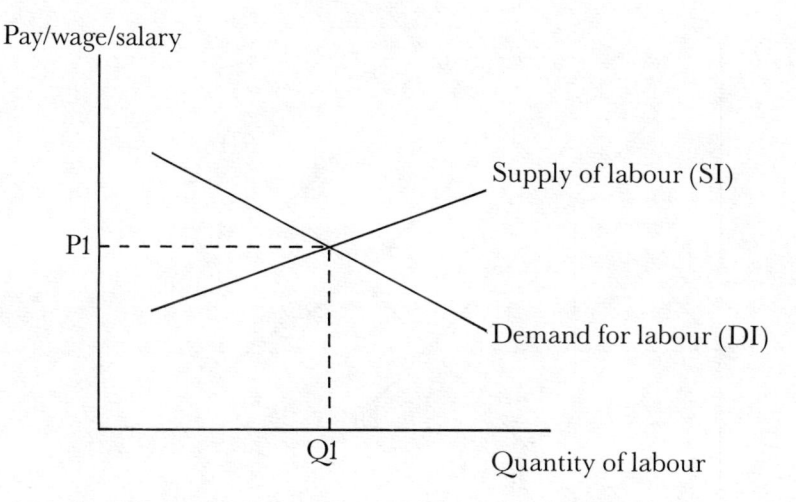

The labour market 1

Pay/wage/salary

[Graph showing Supply of labour (SI) curve sloping upward and Demand for labour (DI) curve sloping downward, intersecting at point P1, Q1. Quantity of labour on x-axis.]

Market curve for labour in a particular industry or profession

It is apparent that only at point P1 do the demand and supply curves coincide. This will then determine the wage level in this particular area of work. Of course, movements of both curves will then influence pay. Thus if a profession relaxes its entry qualifications then the supply curve will move downwards (SI → SII), attracting greater numbers into the profession but at a lower wage (P1 → P2).

Such analysis can be used to compare and contrast many types of wages paid in differing areas of work and types of employment. It can also show how the labour market can be interfered with to enhance wages paid in certain industries. As an example, if the unions in an industry impose a minimum wage, or if a government decides upon a minimum level of pay, the results can be as follows:

If the market wage was P1 and a high wage of P2 were imposed, then the number of workers available at such a rate would be Q2 but the demand from the employee would be Q1. The result would be a level of unemployment in this area of work of Q1 to Q2 (or Q1 to Q3 if the normal workings of market forces were allowed). Of course, the argument is that a market wage of P1 is too low to provide a reasonable standard of living and that P2 is the only way of guaranteeing a satisfactory level of payment.

Fig. 8.10

The labour market 2

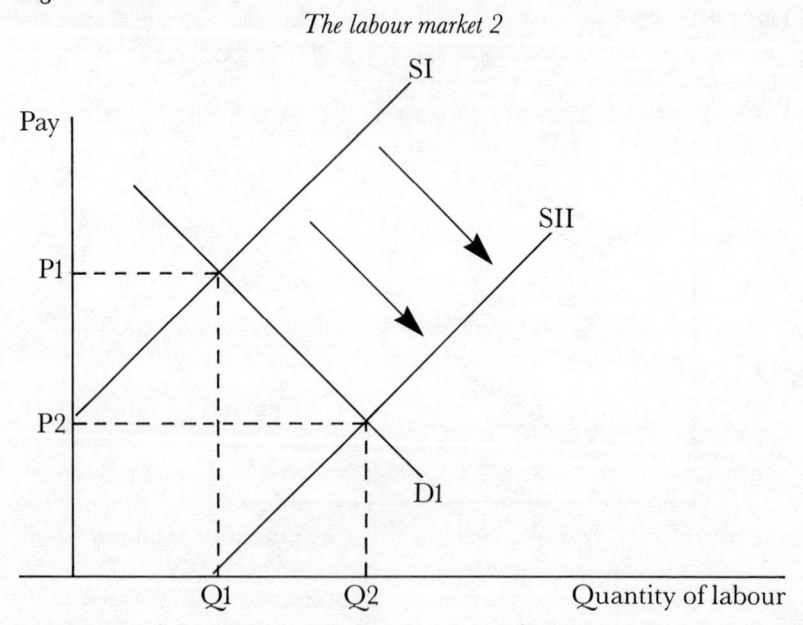

Fig. 8.11

The labour market 3

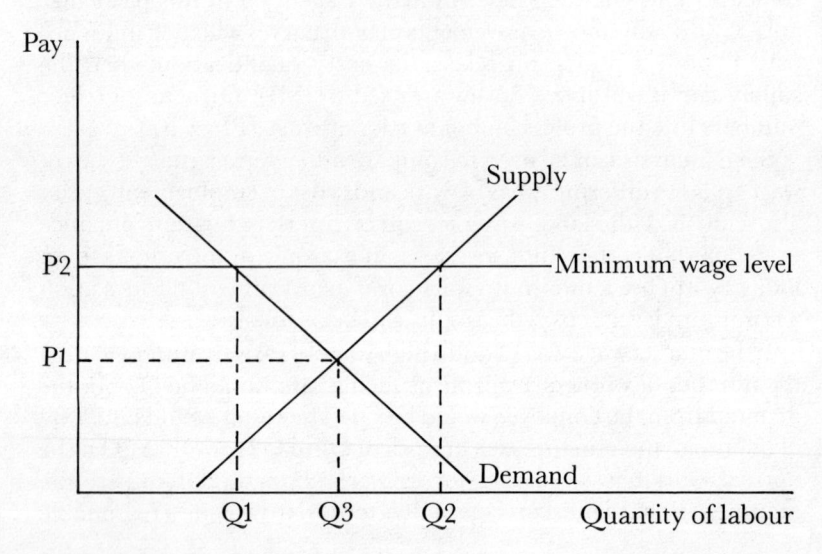

8.6 Gross Pay versus Net Pay

So far we have been looking at factors affecing gross pay, i.e. the total pay earned by a person before any deductions are made. For most people what really concerns them is their take-home pay or net pay. Net pay is what directly affects their standard of living. The difference between gross pay and net pay is the result of a variety of deductions being made. These deductions can be of two kinds, statutory deductions and voluntary deductions.

Statutory deductions

Statutory deductions are those payments enforced by law.

(a) *Income tax* is usually the largest deduction taken from a person's pay. All wage earners are liable to pay income tax. The amount taken depends upon the level of the gross earnings and their own personal circumstances.

All income earners have a tax-free allowance which will depend on whether they are single or married, how much interest they pay on their mortgage, whether they look after a dependent relative and on allowances given for expenses to do with their job. Any income over the tax-free allowance has a percentage deducted up to a higher limit. This is known as the base rate and will vary according to government policy as laid out in the annual budget (Finance Act). For instance in the 1986 Budget, the Chancellor of the Exchequer reduced the base rate from 30 pence in the pound (30%) to 29 pence in the pound (29%). Income over this level is charged at higher rates of income tax, e.g. 35%, 40%, etc.

Example

Assume that the base tax rate is 30%, with amounts over £20 000 per year being at 35% and amounts over £30 000 per year being at 40%.

David Winter, lecturer, earns £17 500 per year gross (before deductions). His tax-free allowance is £5000. Then his tax deductions will be calculated as follows:

Thus David Winters taxed income (or take home pay) = £17 000 − £3750 = £13 750.

Samantha Cook is a stockbroker whose income is £35 000. Her tax-free allowance is also £5000. Her taxable income would be calculated as follows:

Fig. 8.12

Taxable income 1

| 0 | Gross salary | £17 500 |

Tax free allowance	Taxable income
£5000	

Taxable income = £17 500 − £5000
                = £12 500
Tax payable   = £12 500 × 30%
               = £3750

Fig. 8.13

Taxable income 2

0   Gross salary   £35 000

Tax-free allowance	Base rate (30%)	35%	40%
£5000	£20 000	£30 000	

Taxable income

Taxable income = (£20 000 − £5000) at 30%
Tax payable   = £15 000 × 30% = £4500
Plus taxable income (£30 000 − £20 000) at 35%
Tax payable = £10 000 × 35% = £3500
Plus taxable income (£35 000 − £30 000) at 40%
Tax payable = £5000 × 40% = £2000
Tax payable therefore equals £4500 + £3500 + £2000 = £10 000

Resulting in Samantha Cook's taxed income (or take home pay) of
= £35 000 − £10 000 = £25 000.

It is important to note that whilst Samantha's income is twice that of David's, she pays in income tax considerably more than double his tax. This is the principle of progressive taxation which applies to the United Kingdom tax system. The result is that those on higher incomes pay proportionally more tax than those on lower incomes. How progressive the tax system is depends on government policy. Many people argue that too progressive a system can be a disincentive to those on high incomes to progress to more responsible and even higher paid jobs. Often it has been argued that it is due to the progressive nature of our tax system that people of ability have left the United Kingdom in search of better paid jobs or a more relaxed tax system. Others argue in the opposite direction: that those on higher incomes can afford the higher tax burden and should be assessed accordingly. Indeed the progressive tax system can be seen as a great motivator since to increase their real standard of living a person has to take on even greater levels of responsibility to overcome the high tax burden.

Most people pay their taxes through the 'Pay As You Earn' (PAYE) system. Income tax is deducted directly from a person's salary by the wages department, which collects this revenue and hands it on to the Inland Revenue. Every employee involved with PAYE is given a tax code which indicates the tax-free allowance. In David Winter's case this would be 500H. The number being the tax-free allowance divided by ten. The letters indicate the tax category, i.e. single male, married woman, etc. This coding is calculated from a person's tax return, which may be completed each year. A notice of coding (form P2) is sent to every income earning person showing the Inland Revenue's calculations.

(b) *National Insurance* contribution is another deduction taken from wages, paid by all working people over school-leaving age, unless their earnings fall below a certain level.

The Department of Health and Social Security (DHSS) issues each working person with a National Insurance number. Any money paid to this state-run scheme is recorded against this number. Contributions are collected on behalf of the government by employers and sent to the collector of taxes. The employee's contribution, like the income tax payable, depends upon the income earned. In addition the employer also makes a contribution to each employee dependent upon the individual's gross pay.

National Insurance provides a wide range of benefits which include:

—unemployment benefits (dole)
—sickness benefits
—retirement pensions
—widow and invalidity pensions
—maternity benefits
—child allowance
—industrial injury benefits.

Voluntary deductions

Voluntary deductions are those that the employee wishes to pay. An examination of a person's pay slip may reveal deductions made for the following:

- Private pension scheme (to supplement a person's old age pension at retirement age)
- Sport and social club fees
- Union subscriptions
- Company savings schemes (Christmas club)
- Goverment savings schemes — Save As You Earn (SAYE)

Test Yourself

Using the words at the bottom of the exercise, fill in the missing spaces:

1. ...... viewed the worker from the point of view of their economic needs.
2. Elton Mayo's famous work was known as the ......
3. Maslow's ...... showed how a person may be motivated to gain status and responsibility at work.
4. ...... saw that workers could become part of the decision-making body in a firm.
5. The ...... plant in Sweden was an example of a company wishing to foster the ideas of job enrichment.
6. ...... are usually paid to managerial and professional staff on a weekly or monthly basis.
7. ...... is a method of payment for the amount of work produced.
8. Most ...... include an element of basic pay.
9. ...... may include a package of car allowance, removal expenses and free lunches.
10. ...... is a system which taxes a greater proportion of the income of those on higher wages compared to those on lower wages.

F. W. Taylor   Douglas McGregor   Kalmar

fringe benefits   progressive taxation

Hawthorne experiments   hierarchy of needs

salaries   piece rate   bonus payment systems

Questions

1 List the reasons why people work.
2 What are the differences between a salary and a wage?
3 Account for the differences between a person's gross pay and net (or take home) pay.
4 What are the problems to a firm and its employees of having a bonus system of payment?
5 Explain why people's incomes differ. Does the market demand and supply model help to analyse such differences?
6 In what ways did the work of Taylor, Mayo and Maslow help managers to understand the problems of people at work?

Chapter 9

Selection and Recruitment

The working population of the United Kingdom is a little over 24 000 000 people. Within this figure there are an infinite number of differing jobs, each one with its own characteristics. For anyone seeking employment it is important that they consider realistically what they can offer an employer and match this as closely as possible with whatever jobs are available. This bringing together of employee with employer is known as the job or labour market. Such a market can be seen in such publications as the local and national press 'situations vacant' columns, in Job Centres and also quite recently on commercial television and radio.

Undoubtedly in times of high unemployment employers have a distinct advantage as the number of vacancies available is far less than the number of people seeking work. However, any prospective employee should acquaint himself with the formal process of job application.

9.1 Applying for a Job

Job advertisements often contain their own jargon, of which an applicant should be aware. Below are a few of the more commonly used phrases and abbreviations.

Flexitime — a system of arranging working hours so that at peak periods of work the maximum number of staff are available. Outside this 'core' time, providing a minimum number of hours is worked, then the workers can suit themselves as to their hours of work. This has the advantage of avoiding the rush hour traffic in city areas and being able to build up enough time to have an extra day's break.

Time off in lieu (TOIL) — is when a person is expected to work an extra-long day, or an evening shift: then they will probably be given a morning or afternoon free during the week as compensation.

Luncheon vouchers (abbreviation LVs), often used by small firms or offices which do not have canteen facilities. These slips of paper are printed with their value and are accepted by restaurants, cafés and foodshops as payment towards the cost of a meal.

Car allowance — The job may require the use of a vehicle, but the firm will not provide a company car. To compensate for extra petrol, servicing, running costs and depreciation the firm pays this allowance, usually on a per mile basis.

Moving allowance — usually given to attract people to a job from another part of the country. Such an allowance may pay for removal expenses, solicitors and estate agents fees and in some cases help pay for a second mortgage if the person has difficulty in selling his/her house.

Basic wage is usually based on a normal working week of $37\frac{1}{2}$ or 40 hours. It implies that extra money can be earned through either overtime, commission or bonus payments (see Chapter 8).

Inconvenience allowance — is a payment over a basic wage which may be for working away from home, or for travelling a long distance to the place of work.

Fringe benefits is an overall term for a package of benefits including any of the items mentioned above.

Job application

Once a person sees a position in which they are interested, then a formal letter of application is usually required. This should be on plain writing paper and in the person's best handwriting or well typed. An example of such a letter is shown on p. 134.

Very often an advertisement may ask for both a letter of application and a curriculum vitae (c.v.). A c.v. is a method of standardising and abbreviating information into an easily readable form. An example is shown on page 135.

Fig. 9.1

38 June Way,
Bracklington,
Warwickshire,
CV19 1PQ

(Date)

The Personnel Manager,
P. & S. Engineering Ltd.,
Southbury Drive,
Bracklington,
Warwickshire,
CV19 8QL

Dear Sir/Madam,

I wish to apply for the post of Trainee Production Controller, as advertised in the 'Local Review' of 20th September, 1986.

In May, 1983 I left Finham Green School, Bracklington, where I had obtained the following examination results:

GCE Grade B Business Studies
GCE Grade C English
GCE Grade C Mathematics
CSE Grade 1 Home Economics
CSE Grade 2 French
CSE Grade 3 Human Biology.

Since leaving school I have completed a one-year Youth Training Scheme Programme and was employed by Bracklington Engineering Ltd. During this time I had the chance to work in many of that firm's Departments including the Production Control Section. This experience I found most interesting and it is for this reason that I am applying for this post. I am now 17 years of age.

My favourite hobbies are football and fishing.

Mr G. A. Black, Headteacher, Bracklington Comprehensive School, Bracklington, and Mrs K. E. Wolfe, Personnel Manager, Bracklington Engineering Ltd., Bracklington, have both kindly consented to give references for me, as required.

I hope to receive a favourable reply from you in the near future and can attend for an interview at any time.

Yours faithfully,

Peter Frederick Turrell

Peter Frederick Turrell

Fig. 9.2

Curriculum vitae

Name:	Peter Frederick Turrell
Address:	38 June Way, Bracklington, Warwickshire, CV19 1PQ
Nationality:	British
Marital status:	Single
Date of birth:	3rd May, 1969
Secondary education:	Finham Green School, Bracklington, Warwickshire, CV19 8LM
Qualifications:	GCE 'O' Level
	Business studies (B)
	English (C)
	Mathematics (C)
	CSE
	Home economics—Grade 1
	French —Grade 2
	Human biology —Grade 3
Work experience:	Holiday work:
Summer 1984	Linways supermarket
Summer 1985	Grey's nurseries
	Full-time work
3 September, 1985 until present time:	Bracklington Engineering Ltd. Youth Training Scheme Trainee
Interests:	Football—Green Lane Football Club
	Fishing
	Pop music
References:	Mr G. A. Black, Headteacher, Bracklington Comprehensive School, Bracklington.
	Mrs K. E. Wolfe, Personnel Manager, Bracklington Engineering Ltd.

When a curriculum vitae is asked for it is usual for it to be typed and accompanied by a short letter of introduction. There is no point in repeating information already contained in the curriculum vitae.

Task

Prepare your own curriculum vitae. You may wish to use headings other than those in the example. Remember that it should be neat and well ordered.

The interview

This is a two-way process where the company wishes to make sure that it has the right person for the job. Similarly, the applicant must make sure that the job is the right one for him. Very often people take notice of first impressions and so applicants should be appropriately and smartly dressed. Always arrive in good time, plan the journey, giving yourself time to find the office where the interview is to be held. It creates a favourable impression to arrive about ten minutes early.

Often the interview will be conducted in the personnel department, where the personnel manager and the head of department will ask the questions. These people are experts and know how to make nervous applicants feel at ease. The information they ask for falls into a number of categories and those given below are a sample which applicants should be prepared to answer:

(i) General questions about the applicant, hobbies, interests, background.

(ii) Questions about qualifications: why a person chose this or that subject at school; did the applicant enjoy mathematics, etc?

(iii) Questions about past jobs: why a person left, what the last job entailed.

(iv) Questions about the job on offer: why did you apply? Why do you think you would be good in this position? Where do you see yourself in five years' time? What do you know about this company and this particular job? When could you start, etc?

It is also usual for the interviewers to give the applicant the opportunity to ask questions about such things as: the nature of the job, the hours of work, holiday arrangements, why the position has become vacant, what is the wage or salary, what are the chances of promotion?

Accompanying an interview there may also be:

—A tour of the firm and an opportunity to see the section where the successful applicant may work.

— A discussion with people in the section, where they may also have the opportunity to talk with the applicants.
— An aptitude test to see whether the applicants are numerate and have the linguistic ability to cope with the work.
— A briefing exercise where all the applicants are given a task to do, or a problem to solve, either individually or as a group.

Terms and conditions of employment

Once a person has obtained a position within the company then they can expect that their employer will conform to some basic rules. These are laid out in the Offices, Shops and Railways' Premises Act (1963) which indicates that:

(i)   Offices must be kept clean.
(ii) Offices should be well lit.
(iii) People must have sufficient (12 square metres) floor space in which to work.
(iv) The temperature must not fall below 16°C.
(v)   Offices must be well ventilated.
(vi) Provision for toilets with hot and cold running water must be made.
(vii) First-aid boxes and trained employees must be available.
(viii) Dangerous equipment should be shielded and only qualified electricians allowed to repair electrical equipment.

The Contracts of Employment Act (1972) requires an employer to set out in writing a contract of employment. This will specify the job title, hours of work, holidays, period of notice of termination of employment, etc. It is usual for the employee to sign the document and to keep a copy of it, or at least to be able to gain access to it.

Task

Draw up a contract of employment for a job with which you are familiar. This could be your present job, a part-time job you may have had, a friend's or parent's job. The wording should be as concise as possible.

The Offices, Shops and Railways' Premises Act had little effect on people working in factories, but the 1974 Health and Safety at Work Act covered this area. The Act makes the employer responsible to ensure that working conditions are as safe as possible. It sets down rules for the maintenance and safety of machinery and equipment. It also makes the employee partly responsible for taking reasonable care for the safety of themselves and other workers. Thus the employer on a building site will provide safety helmets but he will expect the employees to use them properly.

While these acts lay down the minimum legal requirements, most firms recognise that good working conditions help to produce happy and more efficient employees. They therefore often provide facilities which are better than those required by law.

9.2 Induction, Training and Staff Development

In the past a person, on leaving school, was often able to seek further qualifications in a particular job or career. Once skilled at their profession the person worked often until retirement age within this career, sometimes with the same company. During the 1980s this pattern has changed with the emergence of the new technologies. These have replaced many of the old skilled occupations with new machinery which can do the work. The result has been the development of a wide range of retraining schemes to fit workers for the new types of jobs which may become available. It is also recognised that a school-leaver may need to change career direction a number of times during his or her working life, to accommodate the fast-changing working environment. Many types of training are now available.

Pre-vocational education

This is pursued at schools and colleges, usually at post-16 years of age. Students are given the opportunity to follow a range of vocational subjects, such as bricklaying, car maintenance, decorating, office work, etc. This gives young people an insight into a wide range of work experience which the student can try without long-term commitment. This course of work is known as the Certificate of Pre-Vocational Education (CPVE) and is combined with continued study in mathematics, English and economic literacy. Usually the student will also be given work experience with a local firm. Pre-vocational courses such as these are an attempt to bridge the gap between full-time education and employment.

Apprenticeships

Apprenticeships are offered in technical craft and business careers. The apprentice, usually at the age of sixteen, makes a commitment to follow a course of skilled training and further study for a period of between three and five years. At the end of this time the apprentice is a 'time-served' man, able to join the shop floor or office as a skilled worker. Apprenticeships are not as common as before due to a number of factors:

(i) The expense of training.
(ii) The length of commitment by both the apprentice and the company.
(iii) The reduction in the need for skilled workers.
(iv) The new flexibility which is required of the young workforce.

Induction

Induction is a short period of training often in a semi-skilled or unskilled job. The trainee may be given a few hours to watch an experienced operator perform the task and then be expected to carry out the job itself. Many firms now have induction programmes whereby a worker can perform a number of tasks within the organisation. This is common in many of the large supermarket chains, where — using videos and programmes of work — a person can be trained to be a cash-till operative, a shelf stacker, a fresh food handler, etc. Such a range of tasks gives the stores management a far wider degree of flexibility when deploying its staff.

Staff development

Staff development used to be just for the company's management, but is now seen as an important aspect of most organisations. It is a combination of residential courses and on the job training which gives an employee the opportunity to progress in the firm's hierarchy. Rather than learning the work involved in a promoted job, the employee can be equipped with many of the skills required of the post before being formally appointed. It gives the firm's senior management the opportunity to review the prospects of the junior management in a variety of situations, without making the costly mistake of promoting an unsuitable candidate.

Large companies will have their own staff development facilities, often centred upon a sizeable house where courses can take place, away from the work situation. Smaller firms will often hire a firm of staff development consultants who are experts in that field.

Retraining schemes

Retraining schemes are often financed by local authorities, or more commonly with government funds, through the Manpower Services Commission (MSC). The purpose of retraining is to identify in which skills labour shortages may occur and to retrain unemployed workers into these skills. Retraining is assessed on how successful a trainee is in finding a job in his newly acquired skill. Many have found new employment opportunities but large numbers have been disappointed. It is often the case that retraining schemes which take place in areas of high unemployment do not find jobs for their trainees even in the newly emerging areas of employment.

Youth Training Scheme

Youth Training Scheme is a two-year scheme which any school-leaver can apply to join. Rather like CPVE it is aimed at providing flexible job opportunities for young people. Job training combined with part-time study is a feature of YTS. The trainee is taken on by a firm or organisation, wages are paid by the MSC and exceed the amount a person of the same age would receive through unemployment and supplementary benefits. Many trainees, at the end of the course, are given employment by the firm, who now bear the cost of the person's wage. Critics of the YTS argue that it is a method of disguising the extent of youth unemployment. It is also a sad fact that some trainees, after performing well during their training, are not then employed by the host firm. Such firms may simply recruit more trainees through the YTS without ever having to finance their wages.

9.3 Promotion and Appraisal

We have seen in Chapter 3 how a hierarchical system of management exists in most business organisations. Such a system requires people who can move into managerial positions. Such movement requires both a system of appraisal within the firm and leadership qualities in the individual.

Case Example

Stephanie Dual worked for a large engineering firm; she was academically well qualified with an engineering degree. Stephanie was recruited along with twenty other graduates some five years' ago and was employed in the firm's research and development division. She was trained to do the task of a research officer. Her results were good and she became very competent at her job. She also became restless for a change. She began to set her sights on being a senior research officer, responsible for a team of fifteen highly qualified engineers.

The firm's managers had been impressed with her work and the way she got on with her fellow workers and senior managers. Last year she had been sent away on a residential course at the firm's training centre in the Lake District. The course was called 'Into management' and she was faced with a range of situations where she had to make decisions which would affect many people in the firm. At the end of the course she was interviewed by one of the firm's directors. He reported that she had been singled out as a person who should move to a more senior position within the firm. He informed her that she would be appraised by her own manager and he would be given a clear outline of her strengths and weaknesses. She was also to be given a series of objectives showing how she could improve upon her own performance.

Stephanie is now awaiting the outcome of her appraisal. This involved a long discussion with her boss, some three months' ago.

Her boss outlined her strengths as:

—a good communicator
—leads by example
—gets the task done, even in her own time
—can motivate others
—sets high standards for herself

Stephanie was most pleased with this analysis but was also made aware of her weaknesses:

—fails to plan work effectively in the long term
—too personally involved in projects
—does not delegate effectively

Her manager then set some very clear objectives which she was to attempt to achieve within the next three months:

—she must finish the rotary spindle project
—she must keep her project budget to within £8000 for the next quarter
—she must train up Mark French to take over some of the more repetitive jobs in her section

Such a case study illustrates how promotion with a large organisation can take place, involving a very formal system of both training and appraisal. Such appraisal and assessment is now a common feature of management systems. Each worker is interviewed usually by a more senior person than their immediate boss. The interview will have a detailed record of the person's performance. After discussion and negotiation both parties will sign the document, leaving the person with a series of objectives and tasks to be completed by the time of the next appraisal interview.

Such a system, whilst being time-consuming has been found to be a great motivator; each worker being made aware of how management sees that person. It is often during this appraisal that the person will be made aware of their annual salary increase in recognition of their strengths.

Task

Under the headings of 'strengths', 'weaknesses' and 'future objectives', draw up an appraisal document for yourself. Be as honest as you can. At the same time ask a friend who knows you well to write about you under the same headings. Compare the two results. Can you draw any conclusions about how others see you? Which of the two documents do you think is the most accurate?

While appraisal systems are becoming a common feature of management, promotion to higher positions can also take place in a more haphazard and less objective manner with equal success. Let us take a few examples:

(i) Promotion due to age, length of service and experience.
(ii) Promotion due to retirement, death or a person leaving the firm.
(iii) Promotion through the creation of a new department or new job in the firm.
(iv) Promotion through reorganisation of the company.
(v) Promotion through moving to another firm.
(vi) Promotion due to incompetence! There are indeed examples of people who have been removed from a position in a firm to a higher grade where their influence upon other workers may be lessened.

9.4 Leadership

Promotion into management positions at whatever level, requires leadership qualities of the individual. There is no particular formula for leadership; we can all think of examples of leaders who are loud and aggressive and others who are quiet and persuasive.

Task

Make a list of twelve qualities which you think are needed for a person to be a good leader. Now try and put this list into some kind of order;

the most important at the top. Compare this with the list of a class colleague: which list do you think is the most valid? Do the lists look similar in any way?

What makes a leader?

Recent studies have been carried out on leaders and a number of features emerge about leadership qualities. They include:

(i) Proven ability in their own field of work.
(ii) Intelligence, though not necessarily academic brilliance.
(iii) Plenty of energy and staying power.
(iv) Confidence and decisiveness.
(v) Good judgement.
(vi) Powers of persuasion.
(vii) Working well with others.
(viii) Quick and accurate interpretation of situations.

Task

Compare the points given above with a leader you know. This could be a headteacher, your own boss, the chairperson of a club or society to which you belong. How many of these characteristics does this person have? Can you order the points with the most important ones at the top?

Styles of leadership

Having seen what makes a good leader, we now need to examine the various styles of leadership. Much of the work concerning leadership styles was carried out by three researchers, Lewin, Lippitt and White. Their early work involved observing adult leaders in a boy's club. Since their early work in the 1940s much more evidence has shown how accurate their observations were. The Lewin, Lippitt and White research identified three essential styles of leadership, autocratic (or authoritarian), democratic (or participative) and laissez-faire (or let them get on with it) leadership.

Autocratic or authoritarian leadership comes from the type of person who makes his own plans, giving orders and insisting upon their completion. He tells people exactly how tasks are done but not why they should be done in this manner. He distances himself from the group keeping himself above personal feelings for the group.

Fig. 9.3

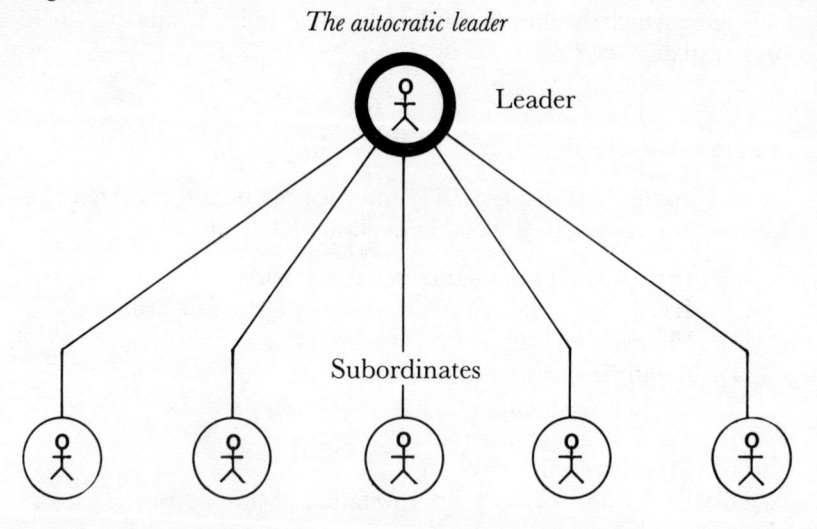

The autocratic leader

Leader

Subordinates

Fig. 9.3 illustrates a very straightforward system of control where each person is directly responsible and accountable to the leader.

The results of such a style of leadership are that the group becomes very dependent on the leader. The group does not work together but merely through the leader and is rarely involved in decision making. As members of the group see themselves as subservient and unimportant they do not have a high regard for their work.

The *democratic* or *participative* leader allows tasks to be delegated and shared. Each member of the group helps to make and carry out the decisions. People within the group work closely with colleagues, discussing the best course of action. The leader motivates by encouraging the full contribution of all members, whom he praises for their performance.

The results of such a style are that there is no great dependency on the leader, that the group feels united by a common cause. The members are more responsible for the outcome and their work is often of a higher quality.

The *laissez faire*, or let them get on with it, leader can be identified as one who feels that people should be allowed to get on with the tasks themselves. It assumes that the group will learn by its own mistakes. Group members will eventually sort out what has to be done and they do not require any control from the leader. If it works this system can be very effective but often such a style results in anarchy and chaos.

From the three styles it can be seen that three extremes exist. The

Fig. 9.4

The participative leader

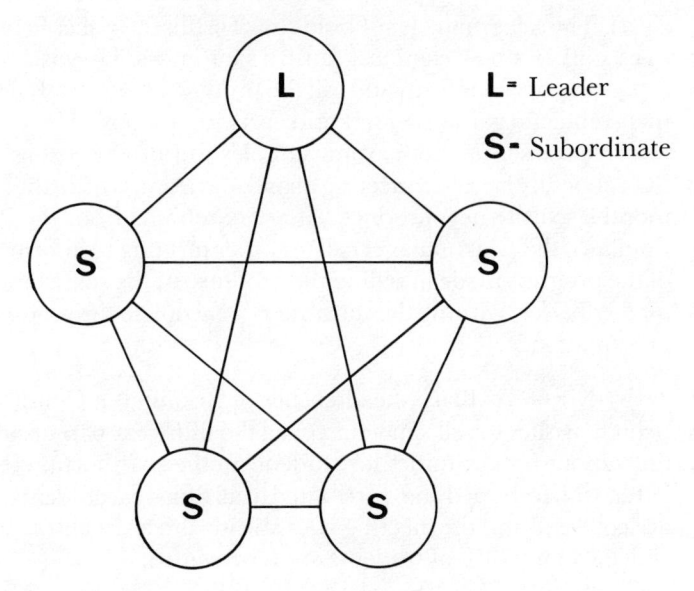

```
        L
      / | \
     /  |  \
    S---+---S
    |\ /|\ /|
    | X | X |
    |/ \|/ \|
    S---+---S
```

L = Leader
S = Subordinate

good leader is the person who can use all three styles, knowing the appropriate time and situation for each. Known as style versatility, it is a feature of the most successful leaders.

Task

Consider a leader that you know well (headteacher, manager, organiser of a club or society of which you are a member). Using the information above can you identify the person's management style? Can you give examples of when the person has been autocratic, when democratic and when laissez faire?

9.5 Communication

In businesses of all sizes, effective and efficient communication is needed. It is the lifeblood of an organisation. Without good communication chaos would ensue. People would not know what to do, when to do it and how it should be done. Business would be reduced to a shambles of people constantly requiring more information to get a task done. You may be acquainted with an organisation where communication is bad but it is unlikely that you know of an organisation where communication is non-existent.

What then are the essential features of a communications system? Let us consider the following case examples:

(a) The sales manager of Boldgrow Fertilisers wishes to inform his sales staff of a new chemical fertiliser for lawns. He wishes his sales representative to inform and sell the product known as 'Boldlawn' to their retailers (garden centres and gardening shops). He prepares an information sheet, obtains some samples and an advertising handout. Subsequently he calls a meeting of the sales team, who in the following months sell the new product. After six months from the launch of Boldlawn the sales manager calls another meeting to inform the team of the progress made in selling the product. At the same time he calls for feedback regarding the consumers' reaction to the product and its presentation.

(b) Mr G. A. Black, headteacher of Bridlington Comprehensive School, wishes to call a meeting of all the fifth-year parents to explain the various opportunities for students in the sixth-form. He drafts a letter, which is typed and distributed to all fifth-year students. Returns are collected and the meeting goes ahead with a sizeable attendance. Indeed about 65% of students are represented.

Fig. 9.5

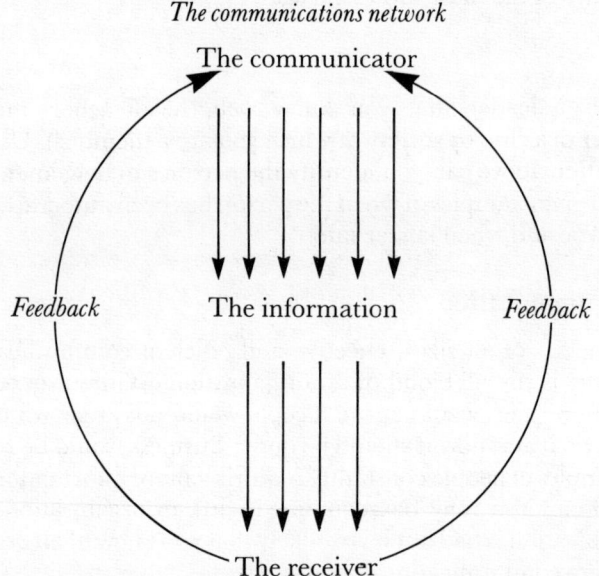

The communications network

The communicator

Feedback   The information   *Feedback*

The receiver

Within these case examples it can be seen that four elements are involved in the communication process of these two very different organisations:

—the communicator;
—the information;
—the receiver;
—the feedback.

The communicator

The communicator has been defined as 'the one who shoots information to hit a target and who gets feedback to know the target has been hit' (Harold Leavitt).

A good communicator is one who identifies the best methods of communication from those available to him (letters, telephone, private conversation, etc.). He will clearly show the purpose of the information and to whom it is to be directed. Finally he will know the best and most opportune timing of the information.

The information

The information is both the content and the method of communication. For the content to be effective it must be in language that the recipient can understand. If the recipients are a group of highly trained scientists, then complicated language and the use of jargon may be acceptable. If the recipient is the entire workforce of a company then the vocabulary must be clear and easy to understand.

The recipient must know why he has been given the information and how it is to be used. Without this being made clear, then the information is useless. The presentation of information may also be important, particularly if it is to be used externally, e.g. by customers, future employees, shareholders, etc. All information must be interesting to be of use. As Sir Ernest Gowers summed up, 'Be simple, be short, be human and be correct'.

The receiver

The receiver who is accepting the information needs to be able to understand the message and why it has been delivered. This person is the key to good communications for this is the person who will react to the information. This person will need to filter and remember the key points and ignore the trivialities. Ultimately this is the person at whom the information was directed and the communicator needs to gain some feedback on this information.

The feedback

Feedback may be as simple as determining whether the person received the message. It may also include knowledge about the person's understanding of the message and how they reacted to it. Only with such feedback will the communicator be aware of how effective the communications system is and whether it needs fine tuning or altering completely. Without feedback, communications and decisions would become increasingly difficult to make and an organisation impossible to run efficiently.

Task

Using the two case examples of Boldgrow Fertilisers and Bridlington Comprehensive (p. 146), see if you can identify the four stages of the communication network given in Fig. 9.5.

Reasons for poor communications

You may be able to see some of the more obvious reasons why communication may fail. They could be summarised as follows:

—wrong choice of method of communication;
—failure to get the message to the right person or audience;
—message over-technical or poorly presented;
—low interest of receiver;
—dislike of communicator;
—failure to give feedback.

Task

Take either of the case examples (Boldgrow Fertilisers or Bridlington Comprehensive) and explain how you would make the information you wish to convey as effective as possible. The following headings may help:

—audience
—content
—method of distribution of message/information
—the message/information itself
—likely feedback
—length of chain of communications too long.

Finally, in the context of communication, we need to examine both the formal and informal channels of information flows that exist.

Formal channels

We have seen that when looking at leadership styles that patterns of control develop. These can also give us communication channels as well. Traditionally these channels were linear:

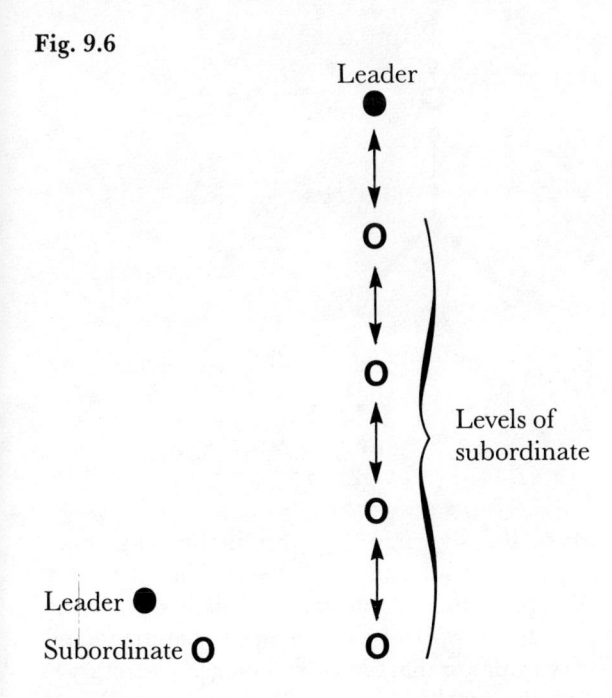

Fig. 9.6

```
            Leader
              ●
              ↕
              O  ⎫
              ↕  ⎪
              O  ⎬  Levels of
              ↕  ⎪  subordinate
              O  ⎪
              ↕  ⎪
Leader ●      O  ⎭
Subordinate O
```

This gives rise to the passing of orders downwards (with appropriate authority) but allows for little or no feedback. The system is slow and will be blocked in the case of absence or incompetence.

To gain a two-way system often shortens the line of communications and allows feedback. Two examples follow, but even these systems can be criticised as they may slow down decision-making. Also subordinates may filter information back to management, not allowing a true picture to be obtained. Incompetent action will often not be admitted particularly by juniors who seek career advancement.

Fig. 9.7

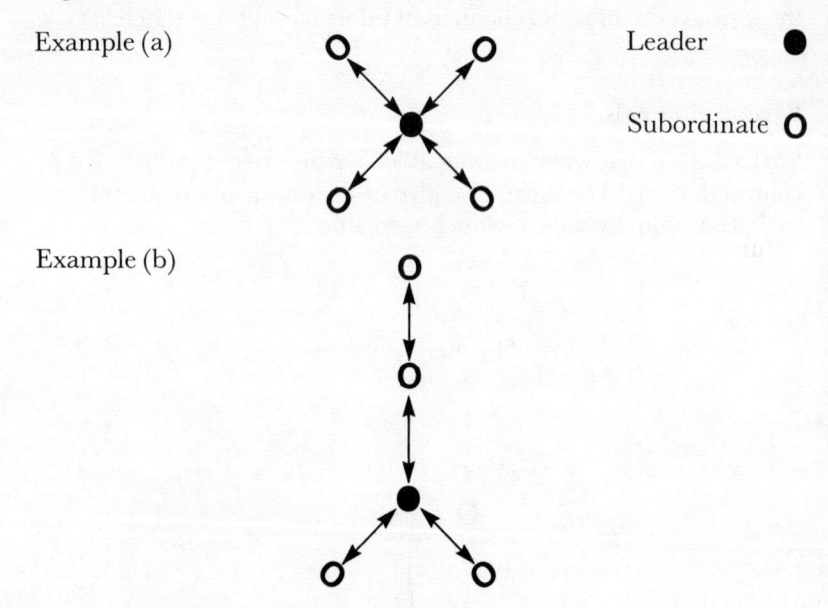

Example (a)

Example (b)

Leader ●

Subordinate ○

Informal channels

Organisational charts such as shown in Fig. 3.1 or in this chapter are at best only a part picture of the information network. They certainly do not show that the personnel manager is a neighbour of the production director; that the works convener meets the managing director for lunch every Friday or that the sales manager's secretary is married to a fitter in the machine shop. These are examples of informal networks through which information, rumours, gossip and the like pass freely from mouth to mouth. These can be vital sources of information if handled appropriately and treated as informal and off-the-record means of communications.

Often firms will attempt to impose a less structured network through the use of committee: the works committee, the social committee, or the sports committee will take people from all levels and departments and allow informal contact. Likewise horizontal systems of meetings across departments may allow a business to approach particular problems in a constructive and inter-departmental way.

Fig. 9.8

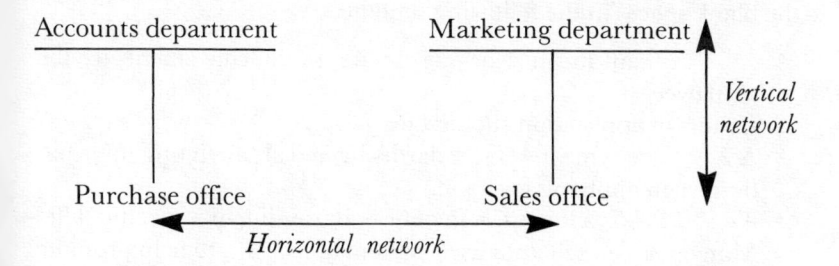

```
Accounts department          Marketing department  ▲
        |                            |             │
        |                            |          Vertical
        |                            |          network
        |                            |             │
   Purchase office              Sales office       ▼
        ◄────────── Horizontal network ──────────►
```

Case Example

Fanwind Ltd., a manufacturer of fan heaters, has a cash flow problem. It finds that whilst being in profit at the end of each year, it has difficulty in paying its suppliers in time to meet their invoice deadlines of 30 days from receipt of the goods. A number of suppliers have threatened to stop supplying them with goods unless payment is made more promptly. The managing director convenes a meeting of the purchase department which is responsible for dealing with suppliers and the sales office team. After much discussion they see a way out of their dilemma: the sales office will request that the payment of their own invoices — usually 42 days and rarely kept to by their retailers — is reduced to 30 days and that the accounts department is asked to advise of late payers. The sales department can then ask its representatives to call on offending customers and to request earlier payment. This cross-departmental co-operation can be seen as benefiting all within the firm, who may now be in a far more comfortable position when payment of their own bills is requested.

Task

Consider the ways in which your school, college or business attempts to cut across the formal vertical communications network. What advantages do these networks have for:
   (i)   the management
   (ii) those in junior positions.

Selection and Recruitment

Test Yourself

Using the appropriate words from the bottom of this exercise, fill in the blank spaces in the following sentences:

1 ...... can mean working hours more convenient to the employee.
2 Letters of application should be ......
3 A ...... is a means of standardising and abbreviating information when applying for a job.
4 An ...... is a long period of on-job training in a specific skill.
5 Many ...... schemes use a system of ...... to help promote managers.
6 An ...... leader is a manager who rarely ...... important work to others.
7 Without good ...... most organisations would work chaotically.
8 ...... allows a person to assess how good his communications ...... have been.
9 ...... channels of communications tend to be linear.
10 ...... networks cut across departmental boundaries and often generate new solutions to old problems.

appraisal	autocratic	communications	apprenticeship
delegates	hand written	network	curriculum vitae
horizontal	flexitime	staff development	feedback
traditional			

Questions

1 What are the usual ways of finding jobs?
2 What are the important steps involved in applying for a job?
3 A friend is applying for a job as a trainee production controller at a local firm. What pieces of advice could you give him/her to prepare him/her for the interview?
4 Why have new methods of job training come into operation over the last five years?
5 How can any organisation improve its communication?
6 What is staff appraisal? Is staff appraisal a more effective method of promoting people than other traditional methods of promotion?

Chapter 10

Industrial Relations

Television and newspaper reports are constantly reminding us of the problem that exists between managers and workers. Examples of strikes, 'go-slows', overtime bans and working-to-rule seem to emphasise that relationships within industry are far from happy. Yet far fewer working days are lost each year from strikes than from the common cold!

Are industrial relations really so bad? Obviously the media reports the few large newsworthy items and not the millions of examples of harmony that exist at work. This is not to say that the problems do not exist between worker and worker, or worker and manager, more that most problems find solutions before drastic industrial action is taken.

At the centre of industrial relations in the United Kingdom are the many trade unions, which exist to represent and protect their members.

10.1 Trade Unions

At present there are approximately 10 000 000 people who are members of trade unions, or about 40% of the working population. Union membership requires a yearly subscription. What then are the benefits of membership?

(a) Unions will *negotiate* (collective bargaining) on their members' behalf. Perhaps the most important negotiations will be those on pay, carried out each year. Many individuals would feel weak, isolated and lacking the expertise to negotiate their own wages. Yet the power of a large union being represented by professional full-time officials is often seen as the best way of obtaining reasonable pay settlements.

Pay is not the only debating point between unions and management: they will also come to agreement on fringe benefits, hours of work, overtime pay, holiday arrangements and overall conditions of work.

(b) Union officials will *represent* workers involved in individual disputes. Disagreements may develop about a person's own working conditions, or concerning his relationship with his immediate boss. To reconcile such situations the union official will negotiate on behalf of the worker, using his experience of such problems built up over many years.

(c) Unions can *provide* forms of *insurance* to workers, specific to their occupation. Such insurance will provide money after an industrial accident or during sickness over and above any money provided by government benefits.

(d) Unions have *legal departments* with expert knowledge of industrial and labour law. If a member falls foul of his employer the union may provide the resources to fight his case in the courts.

(e) Unions are important *pressure groups*, able to talk to and influence government at both local and national level. As representatives of large numbers of people senior union officials will be listened to and many are, indeed, familiar media personalities.

(f) Unions often *provide benefits* during industrial disputes, including strike pay.

Types of trade unions

Trade unions come in many shapes and sizes, depending on the group of workers they are representing. Perhaps the four clearest divisions are those given below:

- (a) *General unions* which represent semi-skilled and unskilled workers, doing many jobs in a wide variety of industries. These are the largest unions and are usually divided into sections representing a specific kind of skill. Examples are the Transport and General Workers' Union (TGWU) and the General Municipal Boilermakers and Allied Trades Union (GMBATU).
- (b) *Industrial unions* represent many of the workers in a particular industry whatever the level of their work. This type of union has the advantage of representing the collective interests of a single industry and can negotiate with the management of such industries at one instance. Two examples of such unions are the National Union of Mineworkers (NUM) and the Union of Post Office Workers.
- (c) *Craft unions* are much smaller unions, representing a particular kind of skilled worker, whichever industry they may be in. These unions arose from the old craft guilds and many have

now been taken over by the larger general unions. Examples are the National Society of Metal Mechanics and the Military and Orchestral Musical Instrument Makers' Trade Society.
(d) *White collar unions* are the newest type of unions, representing clerical, office and managerial staff. They have been the main growth area within the trade union movement. Examples are the National Association of Local Government Officers (NALGO) and the Association of Scientific and Managerial Staff (ASTMS).

Organisation and structure of a trade union

On the factory floor or in the office, the workers in a particular union are represented by a shop steward. A shop steward is elected by the members each year and usually is employed by the company, yet may spend much of his time on union business.

The type of problems the steward faces will be of a 'troubleshooting' nature. Dealing with problems as they arise: why did member 'X' have £2.50 deducted from his salary? Why was member 'Y' not consulted on the change in his shift working? When will the heating system in the sales office be sorted out? . . . and so on.

In very large factories or offices there are senior shop stewards, who will act as convenors to represent major issues to the firm's management. The job of a senior shop steward will be to take the views of other stewards, representing their members' opinions and to negotiate such opinions at a senior level. Shop stewards, conveners and management

Fig. 10.1
Levels of trade unions within the firm

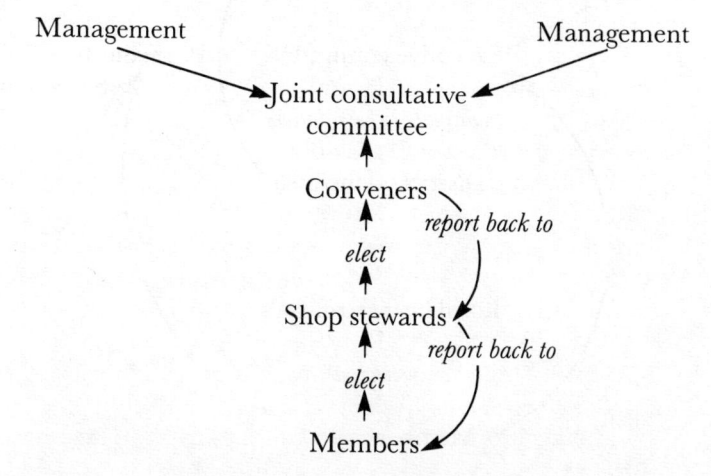

```
Management                              Management
         ↘                              ↙
          → Joint consultative ←
             committee
                ↑
             Conveners ↖
                ↑      report back to
             elect      ⎫
                ↑       ⎬
             Shop stewards ↙
                ↑      report back to
             elect      ⎫
                ↑       ⎬
             Members ↙
```

work together in formulating company policy in respect of their workforce and in interpreting wage negotiations agreed at national level. Consultative committees meet from time to time between management and stewards to discuss matters such as conditions of work, safety regulations, social facilities and dates of holidays.

10.2 Description of a Typical Trade Union

Every union has its own internal structure but most conform to the following kind of arrangement.

Every union member is encouraged to attend the regular branch meetings. At such meetings local and national issues are discussed as well as elections held to provide branch representatives to a district committee. Often at the district level the union will have a permanent headquarters and full-time paid staff.

The district committee will nominate representatives to the national executive committee which is the most powerful force in controlling the affairs of the union. It is the full-time president or general secretaries of the large unions who are seen articulating the union's case to the media; e.g. Arthur Scargill of the NUM, Fred Jarvis of the NUT, or Clive Jenkins of the ASTMS.

Fig. 10.2

Trade union structure

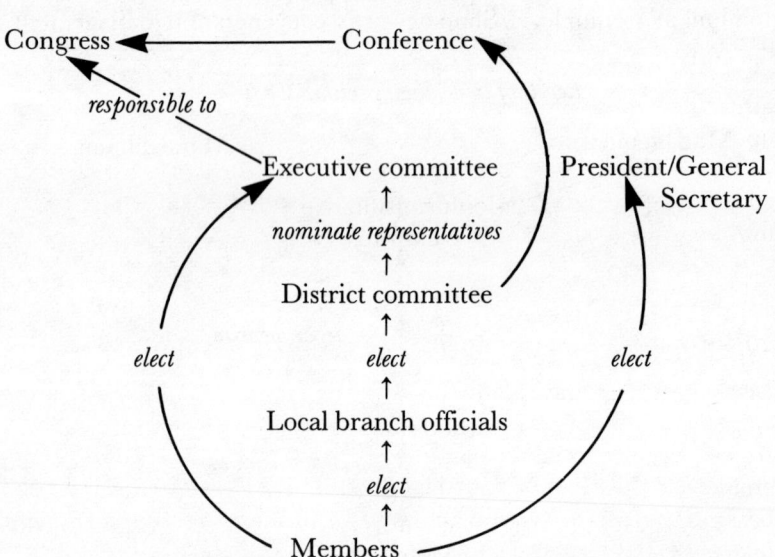

Congress ← Conference

responsible to

Executive committee ← President/General Secretary
↑
nominate representatives
↑
District committee
↑
elect
↑
Local branch officials
↑
elect
↑
Members

elect (Members → Congress)
elect (Members → District committee)
elect (Members → President/General Secretary)

Every year the union will hold a conference and each district will elect people to attend. At conference important union issues will be discussed and any decision made there will have to be implemented by the executive committee. The executive committee itself is responsible to the union congress and if congress (representing all the members' opinions) disagrees with the executive then it can pass a motion of no confidence.

The voting of both the executive committee and the post of president or general secretary of a union is carried out either at branch meetings or, increasingly popularly, through a postal ballot. Attendance at branch meetings is often poor, attended often only by the politically active. It is argued that the postal ballot will increase the degree of democracy within unions.

10.3 The Trades Union Congress (TUC)

The TUC is a central organisation to which the majority of trade unions are linked. Founded over 100 years ago it is a very influential pressure group with very wide advisory powers. The TUC represents the trade union movement as a whole in its discussions with government, employers and unions overseas. The TUC's executive is drawn from the top ranks of individual unions. It holds an annual conference where overall trade union policy is discussed. Resolutions when agreed upon at conference can have a significant effect on how individual unions carry out their affairs. The present general-secretary, Norman Willis, is often seen as a figurehead for the trade union movement although he has no direct power, only that conferred upon him by his post.

The TUC has a wide range of support services, including education, research and advisory facilities available to the trade union movement as a whole.

10.4 Joint National Councils

Many industries have Joint National Councils (JNCs), to determine wage levels and conditions. Such JNCs bring together representatives from union executive committees and from the appropriate employers' associations (see 10.5 below). The JNCs will determine the basic wage structure within an industry, allowing for modification to take place at a local or factory level.

10.5 Employers' Associations and the Confederation of British Industry (CBI)

Just as individual workers are represented by their trades' unions, so are individual firms and their interests represented by their employers' associations. The power of such associations is nothing like as potent as trade unions. However, they do provide a forum for managers to discuss, collectively, their problems and provide some form of joint policy. Their most important role is to negotiate with the appropriate unions wage agreements on Joint National Councils. Individual firms finance their employers' association, which can provide useful back-up resources such as advisory and research departments as well as skilled negotiators.

Just as unions have the TUC to act as a pressure group, so employers' associations have the Confederation of British Industry (CBI). The CBI is an advisory body to the government and its own member companies within both the private and public sectors. Like the TUC it has an annual conference to air and express views and consolidate policy on employer matters.

10.6 Industrial Disputes

In all industries and at all levels differences of opinions will occur between workers and management. These differences may be about the widest range of matters; pay, manning levels, retraining, working conditions, victimisation, etc.

In most firms a disputes procedure will have been established, whereby a problem is discussed and hopefully a solution found. Such discussion may take place at a variety of levels depending on the importance of the issue. The procedure may be as follows:

Disagreement

(i) Discussion: worker to supervisor.
(ii) Discussion: supervisor with worker representative (i.e. shop steward).
(iii) Shop steward's discussion with personnel officer.
(iv) Trade union full-time official discussion with personnel director.
(v) District/National union official discussion with managing director.
(vi) National union officials' discuss with representative from employers' association.

From this example it can be seen that each level moves the discussion away from the original people involved. Most disputes are settled at level (i) and level (ii). Only very rarely does a dispute move to higher levels and this is often on a point of high principle. If however such a dispute procedure does not exist or more likely if the disputes procedure breaks down, then industrial action may take place. Such action may be of the following kinds:

Strikes

This is when a group of workers refuse to work. A strike can be official and is therefore recognised and supported by the workers' own union. Unofficial strikes receive no support from the union. They are often called at short notice by shop stewards. Such strikes may not have used the full dispute procedures normally established.

Strikes are seen as the last resort to be taken only in the most severe cases of a breakdown in industrial relations. The overall effect of any strike is the lasting damage it does to working relationships, both between management and workers and between worker and worker. Strikes will obviously affect production and the service a company can provide to its customers. In companies where production units are linked, then lay-offs may be experienced in other parts of the firm.

Increasingly popular has been the use of token strikes of short duration, which indicates the intent of the workforce and the seriousness of their demands.

Work-to-rule

In many industries agreed procedures for working are laid down in official rule books. In normal practice such rules are not adhered to to the letter. As a method of applying pressure, workers can slow-up production considerably, abiding by the detail of the rule book, with the added advantage of not losing any income.

Go-slows

Go-slows have a similar impact to working-to-rule. Workers slow production by giving unnecessary attention to the detail of the work they are doing.

Overtime bans

Overtime bans can be most effective where overtime has become an established part of working patterns, e.g. the rail industry, the prison service, the coal industry. Such a ban can have an immediate and widespread effect and be a foretaste of further industrial action to come.

Picketing

Picketing is where a group of workers (limited in number by law) will attempt to persuade other workers not to work by demonstrating at the factory entrance. Pickets may also attempt to stop vehicles from entering a firm. In many unions there is the convention that a fellow worker should not cross a picket line.

Sit-ins

Sit-ins occur when workers occupy their work place. This may be as a result of threatened closure or redundancy. It is a means of indicating the strength of feeling and loyalty to the firm. Some sit-ins have resulted in the development of worker co-operatives where the company continues to exist, organised and managed by the workers' committee.

Blacking

Blacking is when workers refuse to work on or with something that has been 'blacked'. This may be the case when a company's supplier is on strike and blacking shows support for those fellow workers.

Demarcation disputes

Demarcation disputes are usually between two groups of workers over 'who does what'. Often such disputes arise when a firm changes its methods of working or introduces a new piece of machinery. The question is who now operates the new equipment. Several unions may claim that it is their members' job to work the machine and such disputes can be very bitter, with union fighting union. Recent conflicts in the newspaper industry are of this nature.

Lock-outs

Lock-outs are a form of industrial action, taken by management, where the workers are prevented from entering their work place. The use of such tactics in an industrial relations dispute is now very rare.

10.7 Negotiations

It can be seen that there is a wide range of tactics available to back-up a union's claim, during an industrial dispute. However, all disputes will require negotiations, at various stages, to bring the two sides together. Most industrial negotiations move through three distinct phases:

Phase I. Both sides put their individual cases. Often, this will show the extremes of views and is seen very much as a starting point. Both sides will know that substantial concessions will be made from these early postures.

Phase II. Both sides begin to move to a more common position. At this stage there will be an assessment of the position, with deadlines being set and withdrawn by both sides. Tactics at this stage may vary from threatening, through exaggerated impatience to excessive friendliness. Any or all of these lines may be adopted. It is the skill of the professional negotiators to determine the precise method to be employed.

Phase III. This final phase may be long delayed but will end in some form of agreement. The delay may be the result of some breakdown in earlier negotiations, or due to protracted industrial action but at some point it will be in the interest of both parties to climb down from previously held views and move towards a compromise, hopefully where neither party will 'lose face'. Such a compromise may be arrived at through informal, off-the-record negotiations. At this stage relationships between negotiators may warm markedly and both parties agree to settlement.

During the 1960s and early 1970s industrial disputes in the United Kingdom became increasingly bitter and damaging. It was felt that a body could be established, which may act as an independent third party in industrial disputes. This body is the Advisory, Conciliation and Arbitration Service (ACAS), set up in 1974. It is a government-funded body but is completely independent of any government control. Its nine-member council is made up of three representatives nominated by the TUC, three nominated from the CBI and three independent experts in industrial relations. The role of ACAS is threefold:

Advisory

ACAS can provide a wide range of advice and expertise in industrial relations. They can help in drawing-up codes of practice in industries, to help determine correct working practices and relationships. ACAS has the power to conduct enquiries on its own initiative into 'any question relating to industrial relations in any particular industry'.

Conciliation

To conciliate is to attempt to bring the two sides in a dispute to common ground. ACAS acts as an outside observer, attempting to persuade both sides to modify their positions. ACAS has an excellent record in conciliation being consistently successful in over 70% of cases.

Arbitration

When the two sides have come to a point where neither will make further concessions, then ACAS may be called upon to 'judge' the merits of each case. It is an attempt to break the deadlock and will require both sides to agree upon the arbitrators' findings (though such agreements are not legally binding, merely a moral obligation). ACAS will nominate a team to examine both sides and will ultimately decide in favour of one or the other. Such a step often brings the sides to a more moderate position before the inquiry commences.

10.8 Present Issues in Industrial Relations

Due to newspaper and television reporting, industrial relations are rarely out of the headlines. Industrial relations problems fall into a number of categories.

Closed shop

This is a place of work where all employees, with a few exceptions, have to belong to a specific trade union. Under the 1982 Employment Act a secret ballot has to have been held within the last five years and over 80% of those entitled to vote (or 85% of those who did vote) have to be in favour of it. In such circumstances an employee who did not want to join the union could be dismissed unless he or she had one of the following valid reasons:

   (i)   genuine conscientious objection, e.g. religious beliefs
   (ii) he or she was already employed when the closed shop was introduced
   (iii) he or she had been unreasonably expelled or excluded from the union.

Often employers encourage the formation of the closed shop or union membership agreements as they make negotiations between workers far more straightforward, dealing with only one employees' representative.

Secret ballots

The 1984 Trade Union Act requires any union embarking upon strike action to hold a ballot to determine the level of support for such action. Before this Act it was commonplace for such issues to be decided by a show of hands, often held at the place of work. There was the fear that such a system was undemocratic as pressure could be applied to the minority and that, in any case, the 'counts' were haphazard and inaccurate.

The government has encouraged the use of secret postal ballots for a wide range of union purposes, including the election of executive members. Cash was made available to administer postal voting but originally few unions took up the offer. Only in 1986 with TUC approval did unions take the grants available and promote postal voting on union matters.

Mass picketing

In recent industrial disputes, including the miners' strike (1984/85) and the printers' dispute, centred on the Wapping printing plant in London, the media focused on the aspect of mass picketing. Scenes where large groups of workers and their supporters prevented other non-striking workers and supplies from entering the workplace were common. The criminal offence laws of obstructing the highway (Highways Act 1980) and unlawful assembly have been used by the police in attempts to control such action. Often this has brought picketers and police into direct and violent confrontation. It is this issue, more than any other, which has brought the police into the heart of both industrial and political issues.

Unfair dismissal and redundancy

A common belief amongst employers and employees is that a person can be 'hired and fired' to suit the whims of the company. Under the 1978 Employment Protection (Consolidation) Act an employer has to show that dismissal was fair if it was on one of the following grounds:

(i) That the employee was incapable or unqualified to do the job for which he or she was employed to do, due to lack of skill or ill-health. This assumes that the employer gave sufficient

warning that the employees' work was not up to standard and that reasonable training had been provided.
(ii) That the employee misbehaved; again warning must have been given unless the behaviour was so bad as to constitute 'gross misconduct' (e.g. theft or fighting would justify instant dismissal, without notice).
(iii) That the employee refused to belong to a trade union in a closed shop situation (see above).
(iv) By reason of law, e.g. a lorry driver who had been made to relinquish his driving licence because of driving offences.
(v) That a redundancy situation existed. This only happens where the work for which the employee was employed has ceased to exist, or has decreased or changed to such an extent that the job is no longer the same. In such situations the act specifies the level of redundancy pay which is dependent upon the number of years the person was employed. It is often the case that employers pay out more generous compensation than that specified in the law.

N.B. This act only applies to those who have worked for the firm for more than one year (two years for small employers: those employing twenty people or less).

If an employee feels that he has been unfairly dismissed, then the case can be taken to an industrial tribunal, although often a representative from ACAS will be brought in beforehand to try to settle the case amicably.

Membership

As can be seen overall membership has fallen from its peak of nearly 13 000 000 members in the late 1970s to a level of just under 10 000 000 members in the mid 1980s.

Within these figures a number of other trends have emerged:

(i) The *number of unions* has fallen from 543 in 1970 to 421 in 1981, with the result that average membership of unions has increased. It is mainly the craft unions which have ceased to exist or amalgamated with the larger general unions.
(ii) There has been a significant increase in *white collar union membership* (amongst office, clerical, administrative, managerial and professional workers). This has come about at the same time as the service sector of the economy has grown, whilst manufacturing employment has declined.

Fig. 10.3

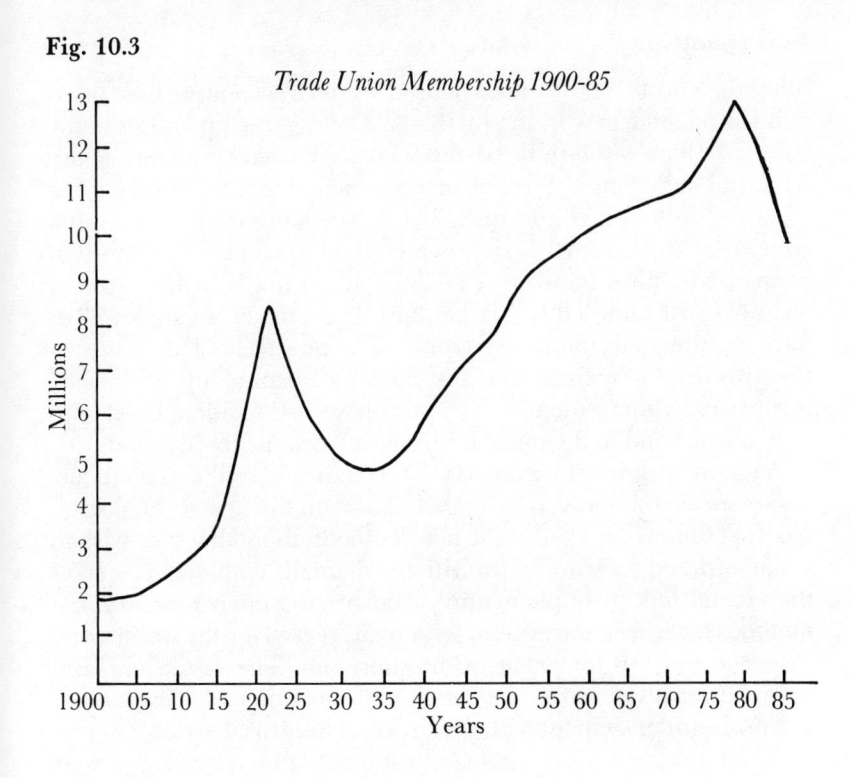

Trade Union Membership 1900-85

(iii) *Female workers* are becoming union members in larger numbers. Such a move has coincided with a radical change in people's perceptions about the employment of women.

Relations between unions

The media often quote examples of conflict between unions (inter-union disputes). Such conflicts are often bitter and embarrassing for the unions concerned. Fortunately such conflicts are also rare, as a set of agreements about inter-union relationships contained in the Bridlington Principles are applied. These principles govern such matters as membership, enrolment and procedures involved in demarcation disputes (see above).

Other differences of opinion between unions may occur due to the erosion of pay differentials between skilled and unskilled workers in different unions. Also the degree of representation given to one union in its consultation with management may anger another union which could feel under-represented.

New technology

Since the mid 1970s the industrialised Western economies have faced a drastic change in working methods. The micro-chip and its many 'spin-offs' have revolutionised the technology available on the factory floor and in the office. Such change has meant that traditional types of work (both skilled and unskilled) have changed. Machines and computers can now do the jobs which used to employ thousands of people. New jobs have been created, requiring a high degree of technological knowledge. People have been made unemployed or have required substantial retraining. The new technology has seen the growth of new firms and the closure of many long-established businesses. Management and workers have had to adapt quickly to such change and in the midst of this have been the trade unions.

A union's primary function is to protect the interest of its members and often such interest is at loggerheads with the new technologies. Not that unions are against the new methods, more that they wish to see an ordered and careful transition, where the employee is seen as the crucial link in implementing change. Too often new working methods have been introduced with scant regard for the worker and excessive concern for profit in the short-run. The result has been many instances of unfair dismissal, with the unions having to face insensitive management with the threat of industrial action.

Worker participation

In Chapter 8 we saw how job enrichment could be achieved by allowing workers to be involved in the decision-making process. The practical application of this is in worker participation programmes. This can be seen in three ways, through control, ownership or profit sharing.

Control Works councils are made up of managers, shop stewards and workers who discuss problems and possibilities in their respective departments. Such councils must be given the power to influence policy, if they simply pay 'lip service' to industrial democracy they are useless.

Control also involved the worker being responsible for the pace and quality of his own work, being respected for his own contribution to the work situation.

Ownership Many employers now actively encourage their employees to purchase special preferential shares in their own company. This has the advantage of the worker being able to influence policy, just as other shareholders, as well as reaping the rewards of his labour not only in terms of his wages but also by dividends returned from profit. The government has also encouraged such development, along with its policy of spreading share ownership as widely as possible.

Profit-sharing is a more contentious issue. Profit-sharing also involves loss-sharing, thus an employee would expect to gain bonuses in addition to his normal salary in high profit years but when the company faces recession and a fall in profits then the employee will have to face a cut in wages or salaries as part of the profit-sharing agreement. The budget of 1987 will provide the details of such a scheme at present being examined by the Chancellor of the Exchequer.

Test Yourself

Using the appropriate words from the bottom of this exercise, fill in the blank spaces in the following sentences:

1. Industrial relations are concerned with the relationship between............and............or............ and......
2. ....represent approximately 10 000 000 workers.
3. The smallest kinds of unions are the..................
4. The union 'trouble-shooter' on the factory floor is the..................
5. The............is a pressure group of the trade union movement.
6. ....are rare but newsworthy items............ are often the last resort in an............
7. A............is a 'who does what' dispute.
8. To............is to bring the two sides of dispute together.
9. The Employment Protection Act (1978) is the law which protects workers against............
10. ....can be achieved through involvement in control, ownership and profit-sharing.

conciliate   unfair dismissal   industrial dispute

demarcation dispute   shop steward   Trades Union Congress

craft unions   strikes   manager   worker   worker participation

trade unions

Questions

1 List as many trade unions as you can. Indicate whether they are general, industrial, craft or white collar unions.
2 A friend is unsure whether to join a union at work. Argue the case as to why union membership would be of benefit.
3 Why are industrial relations popular items for news coverage — both on television and in the newspapers?
4 Why has there been a fall in union membership since 1980?
5 Why is it in the interest of any business to have good industrial relations?
6 How can companies promote good working relationships?

Index

acid test ratio   96
administration department   32
advertising agencies   51–52
Advertising Standards Authority   55
Advisory, Conciliation and Arbitration Service (ACAS)   161
annual general meeting (AGM)   21, 23
appraisal   140–141
apprenticeship   138–139
Articles of Association   23–24
assets   90–93
average cost   59

balance sheet   88–93
bank loans   78
bankruptcy   82
banks   77–79
basic wage   133
batch production   61
Big Bang   85
bonus systems   118–121
break-even analysis   104
British Standards Institute (BSI)   54
budgets   96–98

car allowance   133
cash flow   98–99
centralisation   36–37
chief cashier   29
circulating capital   80–81
closed shops   162–163
communication   36, 37, 63, 145–151
Companies' Acts   22–23
company secretary   29
computers   33, 36, 45, 68, 74, 117, 166
Confederation of British Industry (CBI)   158
consumer   8, 43–50
consumer advice centres   53
Consumer Association   53–54
Consumer Credit Act   53
consumer protection   52–55
contract of employment   137
control   33–34

co-operatives   7, 21–22
costs   101–105
credit   79
credit control   81
current ratio   95
curriculum vitae   133, 135

debentures   86
debtors   91
decentralisation   36–37
delegation   34
demand for labour   121–125
demarcation disputes   160, 165
depreciation   91
Design Council   54
desk research   32, 43
development areas   64
directors   27
dividend   82, 83

employees   9, 111–130
Employment Protection Act   163
environmental health departments   53

factoring   86
finance department   28–29
finance house   79
Financial Times   86
fixed assets   81
fixed capital   81
fixed costs   101–102
flexitime   132
Food Act   52
fringe benefits   121, 133

go-slows   159
'going public'   84–85
government policy   13–14, 64

Hawthorne experiment   114
Herzberg, Frederick   116
hierarchy of needs   114–115
hire purchase (HP)   79

income tax   127–129

169

inconvenience allowance   133
induction   138–139
industrial relations   31, 153–167
inspection   61, 62, 66, 69–70, 120
inter-company comparison   94
investors   11

job application   133, 134
job enrichment   116–117
job interview   136
job production   60–61
job satisfaction   111–113
just-in-time (JIT)   75–76

Kalmar   116–117
Kitemark   54

labour   63
leadership   142–145
liabilities   88–90
limited companies   88
limited liability   19–20, 82
liquidity   90
location of industry   62–65
luncheon vouchers (LVs)   133

management accountant   29
managers   11–12, 35, 37
manpower planning executive   31
Manpower Services Commission (MSC)   139–140
market research   31–32, 43–45
marketing department   31–32
marketing mix   46–47
Maslow, Abraham   114–115
Mayo, Elton   114
McGregor, Douglas   115–116
Memorandum of Association   23
motivation   114–117
moving allowance   133

National Insurance   129
nationalisation   13–14
negotiations   161–162

Office of Fair Trading   53
operations research   33
overdrafts   78

partnerships   7, 18–19, 81

pay   117–121
PAYE   129
personnel department   29–31
picketing   160, 163
piece rate   118–121
primary activities   5
private limited companies (Ltd)   7, 20, 82
private sector   3–4
privatisation   13–14
product life cycle   47
product planning   32
production control   68
production department   27–28
production line   57, 58, 60, 61–62
profit   94, 99–105
profit and loss account   93–94
promotion   140–142
prospectus   84
public corporations   7
public limited companies (PLC)   7, 20–21, 82
public relations   32
public sector   3–4

quality control   69–70
questionnaires   43–44

ratios   94–96
raw materials   63
recruitment officer   30
Registrar of Companies   23
retraining   138–139
revenue   100

salary   117–118
Sale of Goods Act   52–53
sampling   44–45
secondary activities   5
secret ballot   163
shareholders   82
shares   82–86
shop stewards   155–157
sit-ins   160
sole traders   6–7, 16–18
span of control   34–35
specialisation   34, 57–60
staff development   138–139
statutory deductions   127
stock   91

stock control   70–76, 81
Stock Exchange   84–86
strikes   159
supply of labour   121–128

taxation   14, 127–129
Taylor, F. W.   114
tertiary activities   5, 6
time off in lieu (TOIL)   132
time rate   118
Trade Union Act   163
trade unions   153–157
Trades Descriptions Act   52
Trades Union Congress (TUC)   157–158, 163
trading standards   53
training   138
transport   64

trend analysis   94

unlimited liability   17–18, 82
Unsolicited Goods and Services Act   52

variable costs   102–105
variance analysis   97

wages   118, 123, 133
Weights and Measures Act   52
welfare officer   30
'Which'   53–54
work-to-rule   159
worker participation   166–167
working capital   80

Youth Training Scheme (YTS)   30, 140